People are talking about . . . STYLE A TO ZOE

"Rachel understands that everyone wants to look chic and alluring, to look real even if it's in an utterly glamorous way. She really knows how to play with juxtaposition—of eras, of accessories, of proportions—in a way that brings out personal style and looks like it's so effortless."

—Michael Kors, designer

"Arguably the most high-profile stylist in the game gives aspiring fashionistas advice culled from years of dressing some of Hollywood's biggest stars."

—*Gotham*

"Offers insider tips on achieving red carpet style. Fashion heavyweights including Donatella Versace, Zac Posen, and Diane von Furstenberg also chip in advice."

—*Atlanta Journal-Constitution*

"I think it's important to allow yourself to play and have fun with fashion, and Rachel is so good at that. She helps bring out your inner style by guiding you through looks that draw from the classics, but are also so modern in every way. She has taught me so much about the power of accessories, too. I always have so much fun working with her."

—Liv Tyler, actress

"For women who want the encouragement to look and live more glamorously."

—*Denver Post*

"She's become a red carpet fixture in her own right. The sprightly tome has loads of pictures of her famous friends but plenty of practical advice, too."

—*Cleveland Plain Dealer*

"Find your inner fashionista . . . Zoe's book is packed with celebrity images and backstage talk about star style tricks. But she tells readers to took at themselves first."

—*Kansas City Star*

"The celebrity stylist delivers every conceivable tip she's bestowed on clients such as Mischa Barton, Cameron Diaz, and Salma Hayek."

—*Las Vegas Review-Journal*

Style

A TO ZOE

The Art of Fashion, Beauty, & Everything Glamour

RACHEL ZOE

with rose apodaca

Illustrations by Blanca Apodaca
Original photography by Donato Sardella

GRAND CENTRAL
PUBLISHING

New York Boston

Grand Central Publishing
Hachette Book Group
237 Park Avenue
New York, NY 10017
Visit our Web site at www.HachetteBookGroup.com.

Printed in the United States of America

Originally published in hardcover by Grand Central Publishing.

First Trade Edition: September 2008

10   9   8   7   6   5   4   3

Grand Central Publishing is a division of Hachette Book Group, Inc.
The Grand Central Publishing name and logo is a trademark of
Hachette Book Group, Inc.

The Library of Congress has cataloged the hardcover edition as follows:

Zoe, Rachel.
  Style A to Zoe: the art of fashion, beauty, and everything glamour / Rachel Zoe with Rose Apodaca.
    p. cm.
  ISBN-13: 978-0-446-57999-5
  ISBN-10: 0-446-57999-8
  1. Fashion   2. Beauty, Personal.   I. Apodaca, Rose.   II. Title.

  TT507.Z64 2007
  646'.34—dc22   2007006031

ISBN 978-0-446-53586-1 (pbk.)

Designed by Joel Avirom and Jason Snyder

*To my mom and dad; my sister, Pamela; and my angels,
Sophie and Luke, . . . and to my Poppy and Grandpa Charlie
and, most of all, to my life, Rodger.*

—RACHEL

*To my mom and Blanca for encouraging my need to write
and play dress up, and Andy for keeping me focused and fed.
And to Rachel for believing I could do this.*

—ROSE

contents

introduction
dream on

why glamour?

Why not? Sure, as with fashion and beauty or any other aesthetics, the pursuit of glamour is not going to save the world. But life's too short not to pay attention, get up an hour earlier and stay up an hour later, or even to be wide open to all of its amazing possibilities. Life's too short not to take risks. To glam it up!

A life of glamour and style makes everything that much more electrifying, that much more engaging. Think about how we just can't get enough of the brightest icons of Hollywood, past and present. How much we consume stories and snapshots of the charismatic characters living it up in the fashion glossies or in long-ago-published biographies. Or how much, as children, we adored the petite lady living next door who appeared larger than life, a kind of Diana Vreeland figure, draped in incredible caftans and laughing that gregarious laugh.

Glamour can come in the form of a suggestion, a hint—like a pair of oversized sunglasses—or it can appear in all its unapologetic glory, blinding bright from the pile of gold bangles on a bronzed wrist or at an informally chic dinner you throw for your friends at a favorite restaurant. It isn't about fashion. It's style. In my book, glamour is pure lifestyle.

My kind of glamour combines California ease with New York high life. It favors modern, even if it's vintage. It's browned to a deep Bain de Soleil tan and best served up with a crisp glass of champagne. It calls for a measure of *je ne sais quoi*.

Yet style doesn't require gobs of resources, fiscal or otherwise. As a stylist who dresses some of Hollywood's most recognizable and engaging actresses, collaborates with fashion designers for their runway shows and advertising campaigns, and works with brilliant photographers on magazine editorials, it's my job to know. As a lifelong lover of everything glamorous, it's my thrill to share it with you.

dreaming is real

Even all grown up and a part of the global fashion machine, I still love opening a pristine magazine or book and getting lost in the stories and photographs of all the amazing parties and people featured. I study the images. I dream. I tear out pages out for later reference. I admit it's a bit aspirational and inspirational. But it's a personal indulgence that has obviously had its professional merits, too, in my decade and a half as a stylist.

The first four years of my career were a crash course into the world of clothes and celebrity. I was just out of college, where I majored in sociology and psychology. Naturally, I went right into fashion. I was twenty-one and living in the marvelously manic world of Manhattan, as the fashion editor for *YM* magazine, clocking in long hours, schlepping clothes from one part of the city to another, and coordinating shoots and readying starlets for magazine covers and models for editorial spreads.

I decided to break out on my own. I'd already been styling all the teen heartthrobs of the moment—actors, pop stars. I was *the* queen of teens. As it became increasingly evident that I could make in one week what I did in a year at the magazine, I decided to become a stylist on my own. It was absolutely frightening to leave the safety net of a corporate magazine, with its regular paycheck, benefits, and security. But I immediately started styling the Backstreet Boys, Britney Spears, and Jessica Simpson (I met her the day she signed with Tommy Mottola; she was all of sixteen). The schedule was insanely demanding, but I was learning so much that it kept me going forward.

Four years into it, and feeling ready for the next challenge, I headed west. Actually, *we* headed to Los Angeles. My husband (and love of my life since we met, while waiting tables in college), Rodger, has always stood right there with me. We haven't looked back.

Me at age 6 dressed as a bride for "marriage day" at camp. That same summer I won "biggest flirt."

Dream night: Fashion Group International honors me with its Visionaries Award in late 2006, and I get to wear the dreamiest of Valentino gowns.

Glamorous reverie: Joy
Bryant in Alberta Ferretti
during an editorial shoot

Rodger and me

Demi Moore in J. Mendel

It's a whole different game in the marvelously manic world of Hollywood. The hours are still ferociously long, and it's increasingly normal for me to go three weeks without a day (or night) off. Seriously. But now I have amazing assistants who aid in the schlepping and coordinating. I still tear pages out of magazines, but many of them feature pictures of the fabulous women I have been lucky enough to work with holding their own on the red carpet or laughing it up at a party: Keira Knightley, Lindsay Lohan, Jennifer Garner, Mischa Barton, Salma Hayek, Anne Hathaway, Joy Bryant, Cameron Diaz, Demi Moore, Kate Beckinsale. Now that's dreamy, right?

Even an institution like the Academy Awards deserves a modern gown: Cameron Diaz in Valentino Haute Couture.

i was a teenage fashion queen

My mother, Leslie,
Paris 1968

Dressing the part certainly got me in the right mind-set to realize my dreams. I started young. When I was thirteen my friends and I took the train from our suburban 'hood of Short Hills, New Jersey, about thirty minutes from New York City. They all went to hang out at some pizza dive, and I beelined it to a vintage store in the West Village to buy a $200 mink coat. It was chocolate brown and hip length. I had saved my allowance, my gift money, every single dollar for a year to get it. When I got home, I told my mom it cost $40. She and I always butted heads because she couldn't figure out why I needed these kinds of things. Of course, she has always been exactly the same.

I came right out of my mother's womb and into her closet. I swear. Her closet is my earliest memory. As a young girl, I thought she epitomized glamour. Everything about her was and still is beautiful—her hair, her jewelry, her shoes. My sister and I would rifle through her things all the time. Some of my fondest memories are of the three of us sprawled out on her bed. We'd spread out her boxes, the kind you find at the hardware store to organize nails but are perfect for the endless inventory of jewelry she collected. Thank God my dad understood. He has a great eye and instinct for beautiful things (my parents have an amazing contemporary art collection), and he has aided and abetted in her collection, especially during their frequent travels.

The year after the vintage-mink adventure, I went with my family on my very first trip to Europe. Again, I decided to splurge my savings. I walked right into Louis Vuitton in Paris and bought a messenger bag. It draped across my body in a half-moon shape. I still have it. It's just beautifully made.

My fourth birthday in
Dennisport, Cape Cod

The Rosenzweig family on
holiday in Porto Fino, 1987

I was thirteen going on thirty—thanks to my mom as inspiration (whether she acknowledges it or not). And my aspirations and fantasy life were further informed by my hero, Halston. To me, Halston was the great American designer and style icon. He was the first American fashion superstar. I would get lost in staring at photographs in books of him and the chicest women alive who sashayed through life in his clothes—Bianca Jagger, Angelica Huston, Jerry Hall.

His perfume bottle was even designed by Elsa Peretti! I admit that I always wanted to run with the fast crowd. To me, the fast crowd symbolized more experiences, more opportunities. Living it up, living with more wasn't so much about materialism as it was about this fantasy life to be and do. I wanted to dance at Studio 54. I wanted to travel to exotic places. I wanted to do the unimaginable. It was just a matter of "how do I get to that?" So it was beyond a dream come true when I was appointed creative consultant to the storied fashion house in early 2007. I knew collecting all those vintage Halston gowns and old books would come in handy someday!

Halston wasn't alone in my Hall of Heroes either: Coco Chanel, Yves Saint Laurent, Valentino—I swooned over images of their work as much as the tales of their complicated, thrilling lives. They worked hard and played glamorously. What they all shared was an impeccable personal high style. This style sense was my gospel. I was always the overdressed one among my friends. But that's who I was. And since it was my money I figured I was entitled to a mink coat. In my head and in my dreams I aspired to look, feel, and live a certain way.

Since I was very little, I always wanted more in life. Not more things, but just better. When it comes to quality, it has to be the best there possibly is. The quality of a well-made jacket. The quality of time I spend with Rodger eating a deliciously prepared late-night dinner. Sometimes it's worth saving up for the good stuff. That's particularly the case when you choose an item that will withstand time, maybe not because it's a classic but because you'll always love it. A good bag or a pair of shoes or a chair or vase might be more expensive because of the quality, but in the end it holds up longer.

As soon as I was old enough to realize the things I wanted in life, I figured out how to get them myself. I never wanted for anything as a kid, and I'm grateful to my parents for that. But I never expected anything either. I never wanted a rich guy who could pay my way through life. I dated guys like that. The notion of being a kept wife wasn't for me. Success and happiness don't come through shortcuts. I wanted to work hard and achieve my dreams myself.

I always loved the popping cork on a bottle of champagne. In that very instant, the loud "pop" seems to signal a crazy burst of excitement, conjuring all kinds of thrills: stepping out your front door with the biggest smile and highest heels; hanging out with your favorite people and laughing until it hurts; jetting away from home to an even more thrilling place—living it up because you're truly alive. There's an intrinsic charge to those three very simple words: Living. It. Up. It's about being happy, positive, alive. There's even something so chic in the brevity of the phrase, as if it were a synonym for style itself. On those nights when we live it up, we feel our most glamorous, our most confident. Right?

a note from *valentino*

The first time the House of Valentino was visited by young Rachel, she was gathering gowns for her clients for the Oscars. The coral gown she dressed Jennifer Garner in for the 2004 Oscars was a triumph, not only because it placed the beautiful actress at the top of every best-dressed list, but also because it was a red carpet highlight for the house and for Rachel as a stylist. We finally met that summer in Paris during the couture shows when she visited my atelier.

Rachel has a deep love for all that is glamorous and she embraces the new, but she also appreciates timeless style. She respects a woman's own personality when she dresses her and yet has an instinct for what will make an entrance—and what will be photographed.

Her career seems to be perfectly tuned to a time when all the young rising starlets increasingly realize that there is no room to make even a single mistake in front of the cameras. With so many awards shows, premieres, and magazine covers, these women have so many moments when they might be photographed.

In this business, even a fragrance launch can offer a fashion moment. In 2005, when I introduced my V fragrance at the Four Seasons in Manhattan, Rachel arrived with a "surprise"— Lindsay Lohan looking enchanting in an ivory dress from my couture collection. In many ways, Rachel's enthusiasm for style and glamour with these young actresses really signals a time of change in the way Hollywood and even younger women everywhere dress. So, too, is her approach to accessorizing an otherwise classic look in a way that makes it more modern. This is the key to her success.

I have always believed the greatest contribution I can make is to offer clothes that are glamorous, sensual, and feminine. And Rachel understands this in her own work.

Valentino and Jennifer Garner

Silk charmeuse
flutter back siren gown

Michael Kors. Academy Awards, 2006.

GIAMBATTISTA VALLI

where to start:
know thyself. honestly.

Before my first appointment with a client, I've already done my homework. I've studied her achievements, both professionally and sartorially. We discuss what kinds of films or songs she's done and what's next on her wish list. We consider what she's rocked on the red carpet and what didn't work. We discuss what she's happy with about her style, her body—and what doesn't make her happy. Everyone has something about themselves they'd rather change. Roll your eyes all you want, but even supermodels are quick to point out something about their bodies they're insecure about.

It's best to focus on what you like about yourself and what is working for you. Remember, a good stylist is a master of illusion. If you've got a great décolletage and arms, play those up. If it's your legs you love, then give those a showing instead. Color, proportion, and even your attitude can make all the difference.

Oscar-bound Julie Delpy in her dream Azzaro gown, upstairs at Decades, February 2005

create your own look

The operative word is "create." Build, shape, construct, deconstruct, form—all terms conveying a work in process and one that's open to experimentation. When we create we select, combine, invent, refine. We edit. We change. In the following pages, I will provide the guidance to do all of these things—your way. A priority in my work has always been for my clients to become more aware of themselves. I'm not there to enforce my point of view, but to point my clients—and now you—in the direction of your dreams.

The best part of creating style? Whether it comes to your personal look or the look of your home or a tabletop for a party, it's not permanent. It can be changed. Tweaked. Re-created.

And it all begins with dreaming.

get inspired

When I sit down with clients, we determine whose style they'd love to borrow elements from and we discuss why. For Lindsay Lohan we've channeled Brigitte Bardot and Marilyn Monroe as a young Norma Jean. For Mischa Barton we've tapped Twiggy and Peggy Lipton.

One of my personal modern-day favorites is Kate Moss. I love how she can look effortlessly chic no matter what she wears, how she can mix something worth $5 with a $5,000 item. So with her, it's as much about her image as it is her attitude and approach to fashion.

Lindsay Lohan channels her heroes behind the scenes.

Who inspires you? Collect images of your favorite icons from fashion, film, and history. While you're at it, collect images of favorite looks, accessories, interiors, even stuff you might like just because of the color, shape, or idea of it. Tear pages out of magazines, copy them out of books. Do whatever it takes to build up an inspiration file.

Inspiration may also be staring right at you. So much of my style as an adult derived from my mother's style in the 1970s. On my desk I keep a couple of photographs of her from that time. My mom was always very tan, her brown hair thick and long, and she would always wear the most incredible, oversized chunky jewelry. She also had this amazing earthiness and generous spirit that came through in the way she carried herself and wore her clothes.

Even casual, my mom's outfit always had an element of drama. That was a valuable lesson I enlist with my clients now. I always strive for one element of dramatic flair, something that is special about the overall look that we can also build on. I call it the "wow" factor.

When you're styling a look, you no more want to impersonate your fashion icon than perfectly copy a trend. Through the assessment process with my clients (and you should certainly be doing the same), we examine whether the changes in their style they are proposing are what they really want. Is it something they think they want because of what someone else said, or because it's a look that's working for someone else? It's great to be inspired by others, but trying to be a replica of someone else never works. Go ahead and play with the Brigitte Bardot makeup or a Twiggy frock and flats, but do it your way. Be yourself. Don't copy, but do draw inspiration. Interpret it. Otherwise you risk being a fashion victim instead of someone with great personal style. And that's no way to make your mark.

sweet dreams are made of this

With shoe prince Brian Atwood

Alber Elbaz of Lanvin

With legendary fashion writer Suzy Menkes

With Mr. Giorgio Armani after his Paris couture show

With Tom Ford in New York

in my wildest kismet

Successful stylists know clothes, but just as importantly, they know their clients—they know what they really think and feel, and how they move and react. A stylist needs to know a client's dreams and aspirations, her insecurities and attributes, and how to process all that information to bring out the best and most beautiful in her. You have to do the same for yourself when creating your own look.

Got that? Style can be empowering when you understand *your own* limits and strengths and know how to exploit them favorably. It is not limited to the rich and famous. We're all looking for style cues in the way we live. An adjustment here or there or something new (even if it's really vintage) in your life provides a sense of renewal. Even rearranging your closet or the furniture can provide a boost.

Eyes closed or open, just dream. No matter how wide awake to the world I am, I dream.

I dream of moments. At a party. On the red carpet. I dream while lounging at home or running errands midday. Sometimes dreams last only an instant. I can be talking through a scheduling crunch with my assistant as I drive us along endlessly jammed Sunset Boulevard up to my house. Right there, a dream will start. I run with my imagination, letting it play out all kinds of scenarios, anticipating what might happen during a party in whatever complete look I've dreamed up.

I may be very black and white when I make up my mind about, say, which clutch is going with what dress, but I dream in color. I dream in the royal purple of Yves Saint Laurent Rive Gauche and the lipstick red of the soles on Christian Louboutin heels. In my dreams I can actually feel the friendliness of cashmere, or smell my favorite fragrance (an oil I always pick up on my holidays in St. Barths that's a blend of amber, vanilla, and tuberose). I dream of dancing under dozens of mirrored disco balls with Halston at Studio 54.

Don't let anyone tell you otherwise: dreaming is absolutely a required activity.

Eyes closed or open, just dream.

mother of invention

The high life doesn't have to mean high ticket. There are ways to score the good stuff and not pay full price. You just need to be creative. These days there are so many ways to find quality at accessible prices, from eBay to second-hand shops. I'll see a giant pair of enamel earrings—earrings worth maybe five bucks, if that—and imagine them as the perfect finish to the most amazing of date outfits.

You don't have to be a celebrity either to borrow. Nor does a loan have to come from a designer. You and your sister or a cousin or friend can share jewelry or a party dress. And dreaming with someone else always doubles the fun.

Some of the most stylish glamazons are living it up on a dime. They just know how to reinvent a look with a belt or by wearing their hair another way.

Some of the most stylish glamazons are living it up on a dime. They just know how to reinvent a look with a belt or by wearing their hair another way. They mix new and vintage. They glide on some bold lipstick, throw on some heels, and wow onlookers just because of their joie de vivre.

You can even turn basics up a notch with some minor adjustments: a few gold bangles on the left wrist; a dozen more candles scattered around the patio; a silk eye mask to block everything out during a catnap on the red-eye. Just an easy tweak here or there. It can alter your outlook. Isn't life so much better then?

I never understood how some people could not care less about whether things are beautiful or not. Even less, those who tell others to stop dreaming, that it's a waste of time. I have a theory: the miserable ones who tell you to stop daydreaming lead pretty sorry lives.

Take stock around you right now. Can you spot three opportunities begging for a tweak?

five glamour essentials under $50

1 Red lipstick

2 Black eyeliner (always with mascara!)

3 Great heels—the higher the better

4 Faux fur shrug— even second-hand

5 Metallic clutch

glamour is in the details

As stylist to some pretty famous and talented women, I'm well versed in the many steps involved in readying them for their red carpet close-ups. It's not just about the dress, which undergoes numerous fittings before it's camera ready. It also involves the right shoes with the perfect heel height, the earrings and other jewelry, and even the bag. Every little detail matters in an era of Hollywood style when every part of a star's look is documented, analyzed, and remembered long after the actual event is forgotten. And if the hair and makeup aren't right, none of the rest matters.

Another detail never to be overlooked is comfort. If I'm dressed in clothes that allow me to navigate my wild world without a thought of feeling uneasy or constrained—or downright unpresentable—I feel like me. Comfort nurtures confidence. With my marvelous clients, I strive for clothes, accessories, and jewelry that let them feel their most comfortable. Glamour should be effortless. Or at least look it.

High style is also very much about ambience. It can color the environment you live and entertain in. You can even take it with you, glamour on the go, when you're jetting off for a holiday or for work. It's all there in the details—comfortable, luxurious, and evoking a sense of living it up.

So why not live a life of everything glamour? With some adjustments to the way you style your life—from your clothes to your home, from after dark to the morning after—every day can pop. The nine chapters in this book cover it all, thanks in great part to the insights of some of my dearest and most stylish friends—clients and several incredibly talented designers, all of them tastemakers who constantly wow us.

Regardless of what the latest fashion trend is, if it doesn't look good on you—and doesn't empower you in a way that makes you feel great—then take a pass. Style is not fashion. As my friend Francisco Costa, the creative director of the Calvin Klein Collection, puts it: "Fashion is fashion. Stylish people might use fashion. But fashion has its place." Style, on the other hand, is what defines you—the best of you—from your shoes to your sheets. It's there in the choices you make, in the quality of the things in your closet or home, and in the way you entertain or jet off on holiday. Whether this is something your glamorous neighbor told you or you read in a magazine a dozen times over, deep down you know this. Now put it to practice.

So dream on . . .

Keira Knightley tops best-dressed lists in this
custom Vera Wang at the 2006 Academy Awards.

chapter 1
excessories

accessories are everything. To me, they're more important than the clothes.

In the morning, I think accessories first, clothes second. A blouse and leggings might actually go on first, but not far behind are my favorite yellow gold bracelets, maybe a vintage Kenneth Jay Lane medallion, or long chains threading my favorite charms; then a hip belt and my boots, always high heel. Five inches to be exact.

Accessories are the antidote to the blahs, maybe even more than a smear of red lipstick (not that the power of Vamp—or whatever Chanel has renamed its best red this season—should ever be underestimated!). Slip into a pair of super-sexy red patent stilettos and tell me otherwise.

Some of my favorite all-time outfits—whether my own or those worn by my clients or my fashion icons—really come down to the accessories. When I think of Ali MacGraw in *Love Story*, the vision that comes to mind is her in that crocheted beret and long scarf.

Nothing satisfies a fashion craving in me more than a vintage belt or new shoes or a bag I've rediscovered in my mother's closet. I can do without the newest dress or trousers if I can get my hands on a few accessories to update my wardrobe. Never leave accessories as an afterthought. Along with a great smile, they can make or break a look. And they always speak to your personal style.

Make a statement with the jewelry you choose.

altered states

Accessories can tell a lot about your state of mind. The eyes might be the window to the soul, but the jewelry, shoes, belt, and handbag reveal where we are—or where we'd like to be.

During the runway presentations each season, even more than all the newly rendered silhouettes, the oh-so-important proclamations of long or short, second-skin tight or voluminous, the choices in accessories are a pointed keynote to a designer's fashion state of the union.

Slide on a blinding cocktail ring, or hook on a pair of oversized sparkling cluster earrings, and the transformative powers are undeniable. You might be in your favorite jeans and flip-flops, but once you throw on a great belt, you're that much closer to fabulous.

That's because even more than clothes, accessories allow you to nurture your inner fashion chameleon.

the wow factor

There is nothing fun, interesting, or glamorous in playing it subtle. Don't be afraid of statement pieces. When it comes to styling my clients or myself, I always aim for something that elicits a "Wow."

When considering a red carpet look for one of my clients, I know there might be plenty of really pretty gowns out there, but pretty can mean safe, and that's probably not going to score a place on any best-dressed lists. Add a sparkling jeweled broach at the waist or a strappy pair of red-hot heels and a vanilla look instantly registers as a "wow."

wild *for it*

I love leopard. To me, the print is an accessory unto itself. A true *excessory*.

It's very similar to patent in the way its trendiness comes and goes, but you never get sick of looking at it. Add a blast of leopard to any black outfit. Leopard immediately adds sex appeal and mystery. It's a statement, and a strong one at that. Because it's a little risky, it declares confidence. It's no wonder so many designers revisit it season after season.

I would never get rid of any of my leopard pieces. I love my Brian Atwood platform pumps. I have so much Dolce & Gabbana, Cavalli, and Versace leopard from several seasons back that I will always hold on to. I have a Dior vintage capelet from the 1960s, a YSL knee-length dress from the 1980s, and another YSL blouse from the decade before—all in leopard. A leopard coat has that wow factor when you walk through the door—which is why I keep several in my closet.

My mother didn't really wear leopard, so I started to admire it by studying images of Diane von Furstenberg and Iman wearing it. Leopard also conveys a very cosmopolitan flair to me. And it is so very over the top.

How to do leopard? Take baby steps. A belt here, a pair of shoes another time. Only do one piece at a time. If it's the dress, everything else has to be simple, in another color, and wear little jewelry. Never wear the leopard coat and the leopard dress at the same time. Note that leopard prints are not always the most slimming, so sometimes just shoes or a bag or shawl is enough. Choose carefully, and play it as a highlight. A little leopard adds an immediate wow factor.

Like an exclamation mark, a leopard accessory—such as this simple sash—provides the wow factor to even the simplest look, as is the case with this summery Dolce & Gabbana LBD on Debra Messing.

So when planning a look, it's crucial to incorporate a wow piece (or two). You can even achieve a covetable eccentricity through the mad mix of cherished pieces you wear. Go from demure to daring with a change out of studs and flats to hoops and heels (carry a big bag to work so you can make it to happy hour). Or you can channel a style hero with a pendant or sunglasses.

I was barely in high school when I became obsessed with Madonna. I would dress up just like her, in leggings and fishnets and boots and rubber bracelets. I won so many awards at costume parties! And, you know, it all came down to the accessories. Okay, and all that hair spray.

Kate Beckinsale strikes the perfect over-the-top balance.

the classics aren't "it"

What's great about most accessories is they don't look dated the way most clothes do after a while. You can wear the same chain or belt or heels year after year and they almost always endure.

I say almost, because there are exceptions. Each season a certain "It" bag or shoe becomes so tied to a moment—usually because of the way it completely reconfigures our perspective of fashion in general—that it can't last beyond a season. You know which ones they are, of course, because they're in every magazine, on every celebrity, in every store, and on every corner.

In contrast, a classic usually lacks bells and whistles. It's often so simple in design that it can endure from season to season. Think of a classic black pump, or a classic Kelly Birkin bag. The simplicity and timelessness of the style demands investing a little more money in the quality and craftsmanship.

I'm not suggesting you avoid the trendier It accessories altogether. When it comes to trendy accessories, if it matches your bank balance and your personality, then indulge. But you're better off with a quality classic than a logo-splattered imitation.

If you can swing it, buy a trend piece, enjoy it for however briefly it's in fashion, and then store it for much later. A really important piece in mint condition can see the light of day again, and nostalgia for it will have you appearing all the more knowing among fashion types because you stockpiled it.

You're better off with a quality classic than a logo-splattered imitation.

Be fearless by pairing lavish drop earrings and a slim gold arm bracelet as Keira Knightley does left, or chandelier earrings with a bold ring as Joy Bryant dared to elegant effect.

more is more

It's true that I'm a more-is-more champion when it comes to accessories. Make that *excessories*.

Certainly like all good things, overkill is just that. Know when to say when. Resist competing accessories. In most cases, a single jumbo cocktail ring is plenty. Don't pair oversized chandelier earrings with a choker. If you want to wear a necklace with giant statement earrings, go with beads or chains that hang to your chest or longer. If it's the choker, then hairline-thin hoops can work or, even better, studs. While you're at it, if you decide to go with the choker, avoid a cinched waist belt. Otherwise, it's just too many tight grasps for one body.

Of course, every rule begs to be broken. Just be honest with yourself when you look in the mirror: if you resemble a Christmas tree with one too many ornaments from one too many trends, then lose something.

cheap frills

Style is more about your eye than your bank account.

The idea is to make a statement—to inspire a "wow" from all—for not a lot of money. With a good dose of aplomb, a cheapie can look like its worth ten times its cost. Among my reasons for loving accessories is that they don't have to be expensive. You can really achieve a look without blowing much money. Particularly when it comes to a trend piece, fudging on the quality is perfectly fine.

There is gorgeous costume jewelry out there, pieces sparkling with cubic zirconia, Swarovski crystals, and faux gold that (almost) resemble the real thing. Some of my personal treasures under $10 are crystal and glass cocktail rings. I have snake arm bracelets and snake belts and large ornate gold pendants encrusted with all kinds of colorful fake stones that I picked up at antique flea markets for a few bucks. If it's a piece of jewelry that you know will be around for a very long time, go for the (real) gold or precious gems.

A good trick is to mix the most expensive piece in your jewelry box with a $5 enamel ring. It can work. Coco Chanel was a big proponent of mixing real and costume jewelry, and I'm not one to question the high priestess on such matters.

Do splurge on the shoes and, if it's a classic, the bag. Footwear and handbags can be put to the test in our daily lives, so quality leather and better construction will ensure they last—and keep their appearance. A black patent belt or patent shoes don't necessarily need to be pricey—or even leather for that matter (although they might not be as comfortable as a better quality pair). But stay away from some faux skins—python, ostrich, snake. They can look cheap.

And don't forget that there are plenty of sources to score gorgeous cheap frills: thrift and vintage stores, flea markets, garage sales, eBay. The hunt is part of the thrill.

jewelry

Jewelry is a conversation piece. So get talking.

Always make sure to have on at least one piece that you love before you leave the house. Think of it as a kind of talisman you can touch and draw comfort and strength from throughout the day.

JEWELRY BOX BASICS

A life of glamour begins with some jewelry box basics. Faux or real, these essentials can go from daylight to dark and can be mixed or layered, or worn one or two at a time depending on your mood and look:

- *Diamond studs, real or fake.*

- *Hoop earrings, preferably one pair in white metal, another in yellow.*

- *A statement-making cocktail ring.*

- *Wow earrings. A big pair of gold earrings can glam up any outfit in a snap.*

- *A strand of pearls, real or the best fake you can find.*

- *A watch. I wear chunky men's watches, but any dressy watch is essential.*

- *A simple chain for every day, ideally with a charm that is personally meaningful. It becomes a signature. Right now mine is a diamond wishbone that my husband surprised me with one Valentine's Day.*

- *A bracelet, be it a bangle or cuff.*

- *A dressy necklace or pair of earrings. It can sparkle with crystals, diamonds, or colored stones. But make sure it's something that has glimmer—and makes you feel instantly dazzling.*

quality matters

When it comes to investment pieces, quality matters. It can also vary depending on your budget. Even so, before forking out your paycheck for a high-ticket anything, get up close and personal with it. Eye it for scratches and nicks. Examine the lining and the stitching. Pull gently to see how the seams will hold up if you gain five pounds. Look for any dried glue bleeding between the shoe vamp and sole, or from the fixings on costume jewelry.

METAL WORKS

In my world, yellow gold rules. I keep my skin bronzed year-round, and gold jewelry works best with my coloring. While I believe you shouldn't be restricted by rules if you love something, there's some truth to how the right metal color can have a glowing effect on your skin tone. Gold looks great on skin with warmer olive, peach, or yellow undertones. Those with more neutral olive, yellow, or pink tones can get away with either yellow or white metals. Silver and platinum play well against skin with pink or blue undertones.

That's not to say that if you have deep dark skin, you should avoid the sleek white silver of Elsa Peretti or Georg Jensen like the plague. If you love it, wear it like you mean it. Go with what you love—white or rose gold, silver, or a mix.

If you do decide to mix, wear something designed with both colored metals. Find something to link them, even if it's the sheen or style. If you hook on a prominent pair of yellow gold chandelier earrings, don't do the white metal bracelet. If you're wearing a rhinestone (or diamond) cocktail ring with a white metal setting, lose the gold charm necklace you wear every day. These suggestions aren't about playing it safe, but about evoking an overall richness to your look by having a coordinating link among the elements. I have two chunky bracelets that don't immediately look like they would work paired together. One is a chain link with embedded green jade bits, the other has a rusty carnelian touch. But they're both yellow gold and have an exotic 1970s effect to them, so they look great together.

BROACH THE SUBJECT

You have no idea how many times in my line of work a broach has saved the day. Nicole Richie and I were in Las Vegas for an event, already on our way to the party, when she realized the dress she was wearing was too constricting to dance in. This dawned on her as we were walking through the Forum Shops at Caesars. We walked right into Gucci and found a dress we liked—a coral-colored, pleated cocktail dress. There was only one and it was a size ten. Luckily, there was a decorative broach on the front of the dress. I took the broach off the front, cinched half of the dress back, and pinned it. Just like that, the size ten fit her small frame perfectly.

Broaches are the quickest form of alteration. They are a kiss of sparkle that can punctuate almost any look. I love a broach at the hip or waist, especially when the dress is simple. Attach it at the knot of a bow, or at the bust, or on a lapel.

A jeweled broach can accent hair, too. Literally pin it through hair that's pulled back tightly in a ponytail or chignon. Even work it as a kind of tiara—think Audrey Hepburn's Holly Golightly in *Breakfast at Tiffany's*. Or attach it to a ribbon or hair clip. Always have a broach on hand, one jeweled or one in just a metal (white or yellow). Ideally, it should be about two inches wide and not too complicated in its design.

with complements

Just as the right pinch of salt can open up the flavor of any dish, the right accessory—a hat, scarf, belt, and especially sunglasses—can flavor an otherwise basic look to perfection.

TO THE BRIM

I love hats. Wide-brim straws, crisp fedoras, a pretty cloche. They bring instant swagger and finish to even the most casual look. Berets are always chic. They evoke Lauren Bacall and Bianca Jagger, or yield a gamine effect in the case of Leslie Caron in *An American in Paris* (completely French in a black-and-white–striped boatneck T and the skinniest capris!). The world still can't help but drool over the rakish intensity of revolutionary Che Guevara in his army beret. I've worn berets for so many years because they're incredibly versatile and easy to throw on (and travel in). Every once in a while I'll bust a beret out—especially if I'm in dire need of getting my hair color done. I have several in wool felt, heavy yarn crochet, and fine-gauge knit. My favorite one is covered in sequins.

Terminally cool costume designer Patricia Fields rocks a fedora with an unmistakable Warhol stamp

A hat is a great solution at the most harried of life moments. It's better to throw on a hat than leave the house with a rat's nest for a 'do. That said, consider where you're going. You can't keep a fedora on all day in an office, no matter how cute it looks. It's just ridiculous. A beret or cloche, however, can work. The aim is to sport it like you mean it rather than as a solution for not having done your hair.

TIE ONE ON

A scarf is a great investment—even if it's a $5 square from a thrift store.

More than any other element in your wardrobe, a scarf can be tied, twisted, folded, and wrapped in countless ways. Roll it up and tie it around your neck or waist. Fold it into a headband or a halter top. Use it to control a bad hair day by hiding it all under a silk square. Fold it in half on the diagonal and knotted at the base of the back of the head like Lana Turner did (complete with dark sunglasses, natch). Dress up your purse by tying on a scarf to the strap. It can be any color, any pattern, and any fabric (although silk, cotton, and other natural fabrics generally work best). A knit or cashmere strip wrapped around your neck or looped and tied once at the front should be more than just about keeping cozy. It can provide color and even personality to a neutral coat or outfit. I love any scarf with the kind of prints and colors inspired by Missoni, Hermès, and Pucci.

Just find a scarf that fits your mood at that very moment—or the mood you'd like to be in. I'm still discovering new manners of tying one on.

GETTING WAISTED

You never, ever want to look like your clothes are swallowing you up. The perfect solution to a billowy dress or top that otherwise looks in danger of carrying you off like a hot air balloon is a belt.

A belt turns an ordinary or simple outfit into something fabulous. Belts provide a silhouette with a structural marking point. No matter how full your figure, be fearless when it comes to accentuating it.

At the waist, a belt reveals womanly curves; at the hips it suggests a boyish cool. A skinny belt threading the loops of great-looking tailored trousers is undeniably uptown chic.

An ornately tooled leather band can infuse a down-home flavor.

A belt can also instantly convey the overall vibe of your outfit. A woven leather strap slung low on the hips can suggest 1970s boho, while a super-cinched waist belt wide enough to feel like a corset can say 1950s.

Like shoes, belts are an opportunity for "wow." There are skinny satin strips, wide patent bands, chainmail sashes, and bedazzled swaths studded, crystallized, or embroidered. There are belts cut in velvet, pony skin, plastic, suede, and brocade. Belts are also a fantastic way of incorporating the right amount of animal print in a look. I grab for my leopard band constantly.

When it comes to pairing shoes and belts, exercise restraint. Either one can be statement enough, so you don't want to be sending too many messages. You also don't want them so mismatched that it's too much for the eye to take in. Go with a western-inspired brown belt and footwear in a similar shade and leather. If it's a white patent belt, pair it with a patent shoe, regardless of color.

There's more flexibility with metal and metallic belts. A chain belt gives a glam touch to even the most casual clothes, so even a casual shoe such as a basic flat or leather espadrille goes up a notch.

SPECS APPEAL

It goes without saying that a good pair of sunglasses with UV protection is an essential in any wardrobe, any day of the year, or you can do damage to those pretty eyes. They'll also keep you from squinting, which causes wrinkles and is never a good look.

But a pair of sunnies at-the-ready can do so much more.

Big sunglasses camouflage a late night. They're great when you need to hide for any reason, if you're tired, or if you're just not in the mood to be social. They make a heck of a better statement than a grumpy face or bloodshot eyes and tend to work on most facial shapes. Oversized specs have certainly become de rigueur in recent seasons, but they are never out in my book. Consider all of the most glam women (and some men) in modern history who faced the public in shades that were dark and large. So rock your sunnies like Jackie O.

Sunnies, dark and big, always look glamorous.

Here are a few tips to bear in mind when choosing the right frames for your face shape:

- *Triangular (broad forehead and narrow mouth and chin): choose frames with a skinny rim and nose bridge and that don't perch too high. This is one instance when it may be best to avoid large, notice-me frames. Of course, if you have the attitude to put your best face forward, then break the rules.*

- *Square: go with slightly curved frames that sit high enough to minimize the jaw line.*

- *Oblong (long and narrow face): play down length with frames that cover the center of the face.*

- *Round: minimize roundness with straight or angular frames.*

- *Oval: anything goes as long as frame proportion is considered.*

Sunglasses can frame a personality, a period, or a style. In fact, few wardrobe staples allow you to channel your muse so facilely. Tiny, round rims are reminiscent of John Lennon and Yoko Ono (Yoko, by the way, has also always kept a signature set of giant black shades perched on her tiny nose.) A classic pair of Ray-Bans will forever be linked to Tom Cruise in *Risky Business*. A skinny, rectangular pair of specs with super-dark lenses brings to mind *La Dolce Vita*. They are also a great finish to any outfit. That is, in most cases.

In circumstances that require even a possible need for eye contact, push your sunglasses on top of your head. A job interview? Stick them in your bag. Otherwise, it's just rude. One of my greatest peeves is how many celebs insist on wearing sunglasses as they walk the red carpet at the Oscars or other awards show (okay, excluding Johnny Depp, who has style immunity). The red carpet is no time to be hiding behind dark glasses—no matter how glaring the sun. The same goes for you on any big day in your life that involves formal wear, from proms to weddings.

And always keep a case nearby to prevent the lenses from scratching or the frames from smashing.

Sole Sisters: Tamara Mellon and me at the Five-Inch fundraiser at Mortons, L. A., 2004 . . . in our five-inch heels, naturally

sole *sister*

Jimmy Choo founding president **Tamara Mellon** is one of the few women helming a company built on high heels. Go figure. We met ages ago over the red carpet madness—her shoes on my clients—and have been mad for each other ever since, glamour-obsessed soul mates. She's counted on me to style several of her ad campaigns (and her!); I've counted on her to keep me laughing during our escapes to St. Barths. Here, Tamara talks shoes:

I'm going to start out by ranking the four pairs of footwear every woman should have:

- Ballerina flat—forever kicky, they can work for evening or day and always look chic.

- Metallic strappy sandals—gold or silver, they look great with mostly everything, from jeans to a gown, and can usually work around the clock.

- Plain knee-high boot—a winter must, and not just because they look hot. There's nothing particularly glam about standing around in wet feet or, worse, damaged shoes.

- Great black pump—low-cut on the upper and as high as you can handle the heel. A great pair can take you from the boardroom to the bedroom!

For all of you suffering from Cinderella Syndrome, there's a bonus pair you should try to include: a jeweled sandal—with dresses or jeans, it just funks up summer looks.

A shoe can completely change the look of an outfit. You don't have to wear expensive clothes with good accessories. Better to wear higher quality shoes and a cheaper dress. When the shoes and bag appear rich, no one ever presumes the clothes are down market.

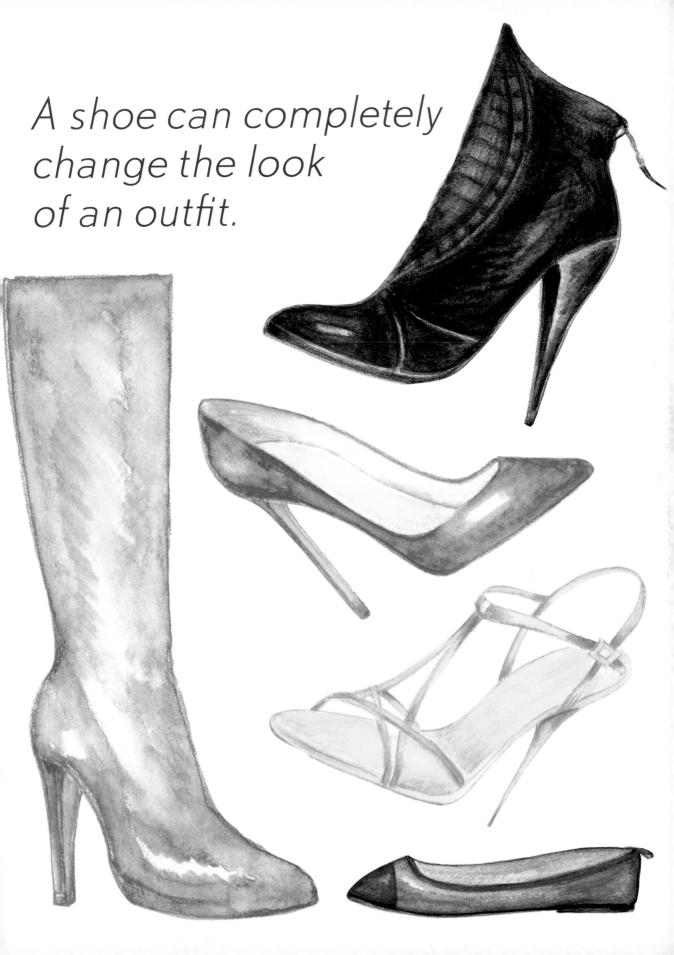

A shoe can completely change the look of an outfit.

handbags

A bag can make an outfit. It can just as easily break it, too.

The most simple of outfits can be upgraded with a fab metallic hobo, a dark green croc satchel, a white patent clutch, or some other bag that makes a bold statement. A bag can reveal volumes about a person. She can turn out in a sedate Chanel suit, but if her bag screams quirky vintage, then it's likely something else is going on in her style DNA.

An evening perennial: the clutch

A woman who carries something dripping with bohemian accents, say, copper disks and tassels on a soft, oversized hobo bag, is showing a more relaxed side. She who totes a very structured, classic Birkin demands to be taken a bit more seriously. The gal with the latest It bag is exposing a weakness for all things trendy (not that there's anything wrong with that, speaking from personal experience!). A nondescript black bag can indicate that the owner is not much of a risk taker.

So what are you declaring with your bag?

For me, the bolder the bag, the better. I love a striking color or notice-me details, be it the stitching, the closure, or a chain detail. I have a predilection for python, crocodile, fur, and any other skin, and I especially go mad for metallics. Go as crazy as you want. Just keep the bags with the major personality away from the office.

Even if you're at the lowest rung of the ladder, a corporate environment demands accessories that reflect you're serious about your career. Leave at home anything too fussy, embellished, hippy, or cute. Consider something with structure, even if there's a softness to the overall shape. It can be leather, a sturdy nylon, or canvas, but try for something that has a sense of quality to the material and the hardware. It should hold everything you need. Stay away from the bag lady look, where an otherwise sleekly dressed executive has two or three too many bags hanging from her shoulders and arms. Not good. If you must drag around more than one, keep it to two and make sure they look good together. Mismatching only draws attention to the tangle of straps and bags. While a career bag can be a point of investment, it doesn't have to be black or brown. Still, go with a color that will mesh with your work wardrobe—maybe a hunter green, white, or even red.

TIGHTENING THE PURSE STRINGS

If it's an investment piece you're splurging on, do not buy the It bag of the moment, no matter how gorgeous it is. You're better off blowing your savings on something classic, even vintage, that will withstand time and trends. A structured black or brown bag, something in a Kelly or Birkin shape, can complement a wardrobe from year to year. A Louis Vuitton barrel, or a comparable leather style by another maker, never goes out of style. Even a black crocodile bag, in real or faux skin, always looks chic.

My vintage peacock feather evening bag is always in.

If you choose a vintage version of a classic, give it a close inspection before you pay. Check the inside. Scan for any exterior scratches. Make sure that the handle or shoulder straps are in tack and not resewn. Designer vintage bags maintain and even increase their value if the original label is fixed. If it's a great bargain bag, try a little TLC by taking it to your local cobbler.

It's somewhat impossible to gauge whether an It bag is going to become a classic. Time will tell. But there are some clues that can help you know whether to buy or pass, and the biggest is your bank balance.

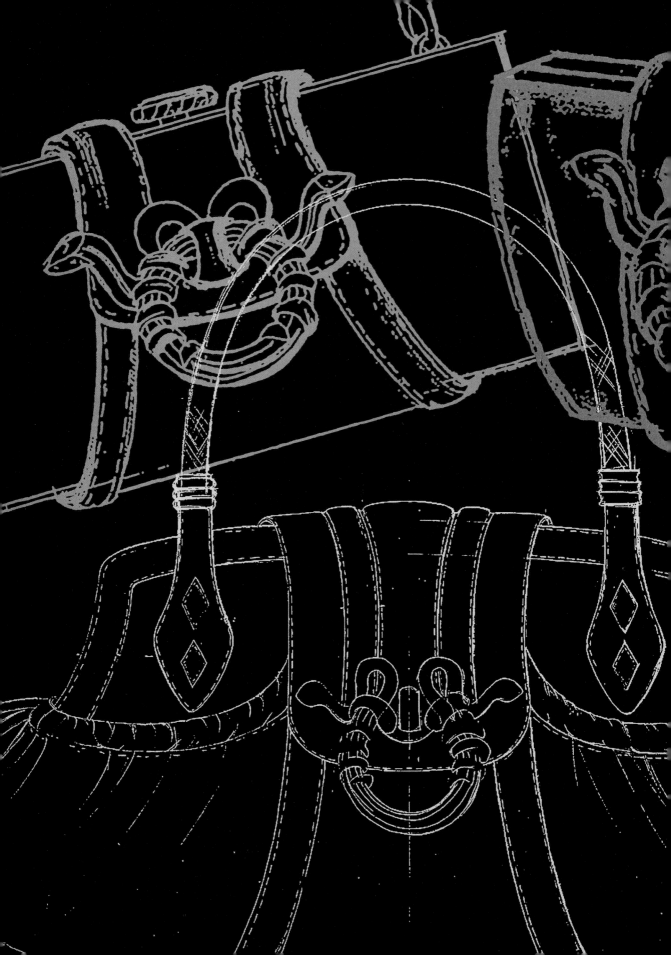

got milk? frank zambrelli bags it

*Accessories master **Frank Zambrelli** is the designer behind several other designer lines, including Leiber. As president and creative director there, he and I collaborated on a capsule collection of über-luxe, colorful bags cut from the most exotic skins, encrusted with Swarovski crystals, and finished with bold, gold snake hardware inspired by a knocker on an eighteenth-century door in Milan. Here he talks about how we clicked, living to the max, and why every purse should come with MILK.*

Rachel and I have a similar groove for the aesthetics of the late '60s and early '70s. It's a high style based in American sportswear. That's why there's almost a casual feel to her elegance. When it came time to work together, the synergies were immediate. In designing the bags, we also didn't want anything uptight or snotty. You don't have to be maxed out to the nines or be uptight. You can be cool and relaxed and totally dressed.

In any bag you should be able to carry MILK—Money, Identification, Lipstick, and Keys. If you can't carry that, you don't have the right bag. But I'd like to add a C supplement to that, as in cell phone—a tiny cell phone. Tell that to Rachel, of course! The girl can't be separated from her PDA.

Certainly a modern girl sometimes needs more than the basics, and Rachel has made it acceptable to carry a large bag into the evening. It is not a tote. Think more of a statement bag with hardware and personality. In the case of Rachel's bags for Judith Leiber, they are perfectly great for day—but probably too much of a statement for the office, with their outrageous skins and heavy gold snake hardware. So think sensibly.

Of course, every woman should have at least one over-the-top bag. To really experience life, you need to flirt with extremes. A life lived safely in monotone is not a life lived at all. Why not experience a little of the absolute superfluous? Have something that reaches beyond your expectations, possibly beyond your means. Make it something that generates adrenaline, that makes you feel 20 percent more stunning. Whatever it is—and a bag can be that—you should have a few things in your life that achieve this!

THE FAB FOUR

There are several classics out there, but there are four essential handbags no wardrobe should be without:

- *A medium-sized, simple-shaped leather style that marries fashion and function. It can go from day to night, and is durable enough to travel. Have one in black and another in chocolate or caramel.*

- *A winter white bag. I'm a huge fan of white bags. And, hello!, that rule about no white after Labor Day doesn't apply anymore.*

- *An oversized tote. For work and travel, it should be large enough to hold documents and personal stuff and go through airport checkpoints.*

- *Black patent clutch. Patent never dates.*

his and also hers

Accessories are hardly the domain of just women. Some of the sexiest elements in my husband, Rodger's, wardrobe are the accents he uses daily to pull together a look.

I love when he dons a simple black or navy suit and adds a beautiful set of cuff links. If the destination is a formal affair, keep the cuff links simple—a silver knot or gold disc. If the event allows for more fashion license, then take the opportunity to wear something a bit funkier or colorful. The same goes for whatever other accents a guy goes with. Think Johnny Depp or my friend Robert Downey, Jr.—the two of them work fedoras, beanies, scarves, and eyewear to sexy effect.

Another way to show off a little personality is jewelry. Rodger loves his necklaces. He generally wears a leather rope with a pendant, something personal. For our eighth wedding anniversary, I gave him an engraved Cartier dog tag. Engraved jewelry for a guy, or something with meaning, as in protection or spiritual symbols, is always good.

Rings are also a sure thing. Rodger's two-tone stainless-and-gold Cartier ring with screws manages to look rugged and refined. So, too, should a watch. It should be able to go from casual to formal, and not be too trendy but rather a classic investment piece.

A simple stainless model with a black or white face and a leather strap does the trick. When I see a man without a watch, it's as if something is missing.

As for neckties, I have to admit I don't love them. But there are times when they work like nothing else. The best way to wear a tie is when it looks effortless and not like it's a noose. Go narrow and solid—black, navy, burgundy, gun metal, or white. I love white. Rodger wore a white tie with his black suit to our wedding. And I confess: I'm a sucker for a short-fringed silk scarf or ascot à la Jude Law or Tom Ford. If you can pull it off—and sometimes attitude is all it takes—do it.

When it comes to men and accessories (and even women can count this rule in), he should always strive to look like he's not trying too hard.

final gems

I'm a bit of a maximalist when it comes to accessories, including jewelry. I layer chains, stack bangles, and leave few fingers ring-free. I go for earrings that can hold their own against my mess of long hair.

But there's a fine line between going to the max and maxing out. If a piece of jewelry or a belt doesn't add to an outfit, or worse, if it screams overkill, then remove it. There's something very wise in that oft-quoted adage of Madame Chanel, "Always take one thing off before you leave the house." To that, I'll add, don't leave home without looking in the mirror.

Glamour can certainly come by way of a simple pair of diamond studs, a signature cocktail ring, and a statement clutch—and nothing else. That is the case with the coconspirator on this book, Rose. Each one of these pieces holds meaning for her, as a gift from a lover or to herself. The "excess" in her accessories comes by way of their statement-making quality: studs that sparkle, a ring that elicits notice, a bag worth leaving on the table at a restaurant.

Collect pieces that excite you, even if it's just because of the dreamy way they make you feel at the moment when you slip them on. It's good to have a few things in our lives that are slightly lavish, even decadent. An *excessorized* life is a glamorous one.

some of my very favorite excessories

1 Circa 1960s Dior earrings with clear crystal drops set in yellow gold. They were my mom's, and she gave them to me. Kate Beckinsale wore them to the premiere of *Underworld*.

2 A slinky gold Lanvin necklace, circa 1970s, with interchangeable pendants—one jade, one carnelian, and one tiger's-eye. I got it at a Paris antique show.

3 A vintage Chanel oversized gold cuff, studded with pearls and green and red cabochon stones.

4 My Cartier Roadster watch. It's very big and very gold. I feel naked without it.

5 My snake rings and bracelets, all of them. I have a gold snake ring with a ruby eye from Neil Lane that covers half my finger, and there's the serpent I bought in Paris some time ago. I have five different snake rings so far. I wear them constantly. To me there is something mysterious and spiritual about them.

6 My wedding rings. I never, ever take them off.

chapter 2
life's a red carpet

what's the point of buying gorgeous things if you're not going to wear them? That lavish party dress. Those twinkling crystal-kissed stilettos and drop-dead drop earrings. You didn't really buy them so they could hibernate in the midnight recesses of your closet, did you?

You don't have to be famous to live out your own red carpet moment. There are certain milestones in life—a prom, a wedding, a bat mitzvah, a sweet sixteen, an anniversary—that deserve all the attention a starlet receives on her photographer-lined way into a Hollywood event. At these times, obsess. It's totally acceptable. I do it with my clients every time, no matter how major the red carpet event. If it's for a charity gala or an awards show or simply a designer's cocktail fête, I want them to *feel* as amazing as they look. Together, we want the photographs that run in the magazines to reflect that.

Channeling your own red carpet moment can do wonders for your mood and mind. I've always held the opinion that any reason to dress up is absolutely reasonable. Even if it's just getting together with old friends for pizza and gossip, there's no reason to show up or be the host looking like you're going to clean out the garage. Leave the tracksuit and scrappy T-shirt for when no one else is around. Even then, it can do you plenty of good to put on a cute dress and some lip gloss.

Dressing up is an opportunity to flaunt another side of you. If it means playing someone else, so be it. Play the sophisticate, like Lauren Bacall. Flirt with seduction, like Elizabeth Taylor. Or try chic as only Bianca Jagger or Diane von Furstenberg personify it.

Never mind who you are by day. By nightfall transform your look—and attitude—and become a superstar. Mere mortals will bow.

Trade black for blue, as Demi Moore, with her love Ashton Kutcher at her side, did in sapphire Alberta Ferretti at the Screen Actors Guild Awards, 2007.

In my line of work, I'm like a fairy godmother on a mission to make dreams come true. Sometimes I even get to be Cinderella at the ball. At the 2005 Golden Globes, my friend Carlos Souza, the liaison between the storied fashion house of Valentino and the rest of the world, played fairy godfather to me when he lent me a gown from one of Mr. Valentino's first couture collections. It was a black-and-white dress with a tortoise print, one shoulder and very Grecian. On the hip were these huge crystal jeweled snakes. I didn't want to wear it because I was so afraid something would spill on it. But Carlos pushed. I still pinch myself just thinking about it. I felt amazing.

To be able to wear such a beautiful couture gown by the great Mr. Valentino was an honor, of course. I'm not a film star. Mr. Valentino knows how to summon that kind of Golden Age Hollywood style better than anyone. He epitomizes elegance, class, and perfection. This was such a perfect dress for me that I felt comfortable and utterly glamorous.

Everyone has these kind of Cinderella moments in mind. Maybe it was a real-life event when you felt like a star for the night. Or it simply exists as your prized dream for a future event. Getting there doesn't have to involve a couture dress. You can have something copied and made. You can go vintage. There are countless options (and we'll explore many of them in coming pages). The trick is to find something that makes you feel beautiful.

Once you're at the big event, you should look so amazing and feel so at ease that your only concern is having a good time.

Selma Blair at the 2004 Vanity Fair Oscar bash, evokes old-Hollywood glamour in vintage Gianni Versace.

why we do it up

Dressing up is about celebrating. It is living it up. It's what differentiates the cork-popping moments from the everyday routine of our lives. It might be an anniversary or a birthday, a deserved promotion at the job, or an intimate reunion among friends, yet whatever the occasion, you should dress like it means something.

Ditching our daily uniforms for something special is more than just abiding by the dress code for the event. It's a matter of respect for your host and your fellow guests. If someone goes through all the effort of throwing a party and you show up looking utterly casual, you're basically declaring to the host and the world that you don't really care so much about the occasion or them.

Your appearance shows your appreciation for being invited.

ready? or not?

Few of life's celebrated moments happen spontaneously. Usually an invitation arrives weeks, if not days before. And even if you only have a couple of hours' notice to toast a special something or other, knowing what to wear should come to mind instantly and effortlessly.

The only way that's going to happen is by being prepared. Don't wait for the day before, let alone the day of an event, to style yourself. Having everything—*everything*—ready

In full color: Liv Tyler in Calvin Klein at the Met's Costume Institute Gala, 2007.

Don't fear prints. Nicole Richie in an African batik Costume National sheath.

in advance will ensure against stress and panic ruining what's supposed to be a few hours of fun.

Whether you have an invite awaiting your RSVP or nothing on the calendar, the first steps in this entire process are as basic as they are consequential: taking stock and planning ahead.

Taking stock is the only way to really know what you have—and don't have—for the party. Whether you can set aside one hour or one day, it's important to know what is already squirreled away in your closets and drawers, in the jewelry case, and in all those shoeboxes. Like a stock person at Barneys, be up to date with what is in every department of your wardrobe. No wardrobe is too small to overlook in this process.

Planning ahead is essentially being prepared. A rush decision generally ends up blowing money and time. We've all been there: just hours before a big party, racing out to a store, grabbing a pair of heels that our credit card statement clearly and loudly insists we shouldn't be splurging on, then to the dry cleaners before screeching home. We arrive at the party a little late, pretty flustered, and most certainly still shell-shocked from the tight shoes.

As a stylist, one of my primary concerns is preparing every picture-perfect item necessary for a client to attend a Hollywood film premiere, an awards ceremony such as the Academy Awards, or a fundraising gala at the Metropolitan Museum of Art in New York. The process typically begins a week or two in advance. We select the dress and pair it with shoes, jewelry, and a clutch that perfectly suit the event. We do any necessary fittings so the clothes hang on the client just right. If a body slimmer, nipple pads, or support fishnets are necessary, we get them.

How she looks on the actual day of the event shouldn't be of concern, particularly when she's standing there on the red carpet in front of a legion of snap-happy photographers. The planning has taken care of all this.

Once the inventory is assessed, it's time to do some damage. I mean in a good and sensible way, of course. Make a list of everything missing to round out your planned look. Then go out and gather those elements—before showtime.

Getting those go-to glam items ready in advance means you have the luxury to find what you love. You might even end up saving a few bills for other fun.

make a list

For all my dependence on my PDA, cell phone, and laptop (and I can't live without them), nothing beats a notebook and a pen when I'm making up a list. Success in styling is in the details, and nowhere are the details better highlighted than on paper.

I am huge on making lists. Lists that help plan out an outfit, a trip, a menu, or even accessories you're missing in your home can go a long way toward making life easier. The best-laid plans may not always triumph, but they can save you plenty of stress. As a stylist, I ensure my clients don't have to stress or worry about how they're going to look for an important public appearance.

Do the same for yourself.

Figure out what's missing in your wardrobe and what needs repairs, and write it all down. Is that incredible gown still unworn because you haven't made the time to score the perfect strappy silver heels? Did you forget to replace the fishnets that shredded the last time they saw the lights of night, and so you just can't doll up in your favorite party frock? Is the double-stick tape holding up the hem on a well-serviced gown no longer cutting it?

Before a big event or vacation, lay every outfit out on the bed, from shoes to earrings. Then write it down. This process forces you to face what's missing (a pair of nude fishnets? A black bra? A purse?). That way, at showtime, it's all at the ready. Once you've done this over and over, you'll find in your everyday life that you may no longer have to write everything down. But when you're away, entertaining at home, or just getting ready to go out, if you put the time in initially it's so much easier when you're in the thick of it.

Keep the list in your purse or pocket when you hit the shopping trail. Otherwise it's like going to the supermarket hungry. You start to buy things you don't really need because you're starving. It can get even worse during a sale. So make a checklist of what you need and stick to it.

By taking stock and planning ahead, the big day will turn out dazzling.

checklist

Like a good bartender, have at the ready these go-to glam elements for the perfect cocktail (look)—in advance of a party, any party. The point is to have these basics in your wardrobe before the invitation arrives so you won't have to fret, whether you have five weeks or five minutes to prepare.

1 Classic black dress.

2 Nude or black patent pumps.

3 Great gold cuff or bracelet.

4 Perfect red lipstick (see Chapter 5 on choosing the right one).

5 Fishnets and black tights.

6 An all-season wrap or shrug.

joy bryant owns up to owning it

With all the premieres and parties I go to, I'm lucky to have access to fashion houses and fabulous jewelry. But when Rachel isn't dressing me and I'm shopping for my private self, I am very aware of what works on my body. I know my flaws—yes, I have them. Size and age doesn't matter. We all have negatives. We also all have positives we can accentuate. I know what makes me comfortable and what doesn't. I also know my limitations, but I don't let them get me down. I work within them.

I'm not going to just wear anything because it looks good. It has to speak to my personality, who I am. What speaks to me about my style is ease, how I feel in it. I don't care which designer made it. If I'm not comfortable in it, forget it.

So I prefer to keep it simple. I'll do little jewelry, maybe a broach or a big ring. I'll dress it up with the heels. Most importantly I work something I feel so sexy and confident in that I end up having the best time. A party is supposed to be fun. You never want to be fussing over your clothes.

Years ago, before I was acting and when I was still modeling, I went to an event as Tommy Hilfiger's guest. I went to give his brother Andy a hug and the strap on my dress popped. It was a real wardrobe malfunction! I ran to the bathroom and someone managed to pin the crazy strap in a whole new way that held the dress up and made it look cool. It could've been a disaster. Sometimes you get thrown into a tricky situation. You can either cry or make it work. And guess what? Keep smiling and no one's going to even notice.

Fit is very important. Doesn't matter if you're big, small, fat, or thin. A dress shouldn't own you. It shouldn't overpower you. You should own it. While I undergo fittings for many of my public appearances, I admit I'm not good about getting to the tailor in my private life. I think, "I'll go the cleaners and get this fitted," but I don't. So I try to find things off the rack that fit right. If they don't, I pass.

Inside Rachel's home studio in L.A.

Polaroids from the fitting

I'm in a career where I'm fortunate enough to wear expensive gowns and jewelry. But I love Top Shop in London and I've worn stuff I bought at H&M for under $100 to big events. It goes back to owning the look. Your attitude and the way you wear it—maybe a few good pieces of jewelry, your hair, and your makeup—make the difference. As long as it doesn't look cheap. I stress "look" because even expensive things can look cheap.

Sometimes you have to sacrifice a little comfort for image. It may be the heels. You have to decide if it's worth it and then commit. No walking around barefoot or complaining! Sometimes you have to push the envelope. For example, white is something I tend to resist. With my coloring it works on me, but I often stay away from white because I'm so paranoid about getting it dirty. I think, "Oh, I won't wear red lipstick or drink red wine in that." That's my initial reaction. Then Rachel goes, "Relax, you're not five." She's right, too. It rarely, if ever, happens that I end up ruining a white dress.

It's important to have good friends around who can point out when you look like a damn fool. It can't be bull or it won't help you. Looking gorgeous for a big night isn't about being a fashionista. It's about being confident and comfortable. It's about knowing your style and owning it. You see a lot of people looking crazy and you can't help but think, "God, she must have no friends!" True friends will make sure you look your best.

A week later, 3,000 miles from L. A. and feeling fabulous in Alexander McQueen, at the Met's Costume Institute Gala in New York

shoot from the hip

Life appears more revealing in pictures, so get the camera out.

With my clients, I always keep a Polaroid camera nearby. Balance and proportion become more obvious when framed in a photograph. You can see whether those flats make you look stubby in that knee-length dress, or whether it's the dress that's got to go. You can see whether the line on a pair of trousers is flattering or if it's only exaggerating your most dreaded flaws.

A photograph can disclose whether a color washes you out, if too much jewelry is made worse by too much hair, or what the difference is between gown A and gown B. In an instant, everything is revealed. Have someone you know snap a few shots of you in a party dress and you'll see what I mean.

I'm always observing my clients: how they walk, how they carry themselves. We mull over how they might pose on the red carpet in a given gown. A single dress can determine a pose or walk. During a fitting before an event, we take photographs of clients standing the way they normally do and the way that looks best in the dress. This way they can really tell the difference—before they go out in front of the wall of clicking photographers. It's a good way for anyone to get the full picture before stepping out for the big night.

A camera comes in handy in other arenas, too. Snap a photo of a room and suddenly the truth is in focus: the lamp cord that would be better off hidden; those sofa pillows that really do clash with the nearby chair—but more about that later. A photograph makes it suddenly, unequivocally obvious whether an outfit (or a room) looks good and if it's really relevant to who you are.

Snap and click before the big night: Jennifer Garner in Zac Posen during a pre-Oscar fitting

strike *a pose*

So just what is the best way to pose?

It's no fluke that nearly every starlet appears in magazines photographed standing in a similar way. How you pose for a picture can be the difference between looking your best or looking like a slouch with ten extra pounds you don't even carry. It can ruin the line of the dress. Worse, it's freeze-framed in a snapshot forever after.

The reason most red carpet poses appear to be angled from a side or three-quarter viewpoint is that it gives the appearance of smaller hips. So, too, the ubiquitous trick of crossing ankles.

If seated, push forward slightly to keep the bottom half farther away from the lens. Bend your legs at the knee and push your feet slightly back.

The standard beauty pageant pose—one hand planted on a hip with the other arm straight down—is popular for good reason. It not only gives a woman something to do with her hands, it also causes her to consider how the rest of her figure appears (stomach in, shoulders back). This has its drawbacks, however, one being that you can end up looking like a pageant contestant!

In fact, many top fashion magazines choose red carpet and party images that depict starlets and socialites in more "natural" poses: hands hanging relaxed at the sides of the body (not too stiff), or one hand gracefully holding an evening clutch while the other arm hangs down relaxed. Palms are best facing the thigh.

As for your face? A chin tipped slightly up can stretch out a double chin. But don't overdo it or you risk an uninvited view of your nostrils. Or tip your head down, and the focus is on the eyes. Keep lips partially open or smile generously. Vamp it up, but never to the extent of appearing like a caricature of a drag queen or beauty pageant contestant. When in doubt, smile! Any flaws in your outfit or pose disappear when you look like you're having a great time.

At the 2007 Golden Globes: Frothy as this Valentino Haute Couture gown is, Cameron Diaz counters it by forgoing an updo with loosely pulled-back hair, achieving a thoroughly modern glamour.

Your friends might lie, but the camera never does.

cameras and color

Famous or not, you're bound to end up on the other side of a lens during a special event. Be it paparazzi cameras or your friend's camcorder, there are measures you can take to avoid appearing washed out.

First, consider your skin and hair tones.

If you're really pale, avoid colors too close to your skin tone, such as blush, nudes, or whites. Conversely, dark skin looks great against camouflage colors such as olive, as well as nude, gold, and champagne. Unless that's you, avoid most olives and sharp shades like chartreuse.

If your hair is yellow blonde, don't wear yellow. There's an entire spectrum of colors you can go with instead. Gray tends to wash skin out, while rich jewel tones tend to look good on almost everyone. Pastels can work as long as you're not too fair skinned. Pale or dark, my clients tend to look best in colors that are rich and bold. There's no great mystery as to why black, white, and red are staples at Hollywood events. These are colors that pop and look striking on just about anyone.

Buy something because you need it, and you

it's no sheer luck

Next step for a picture-perfect night is the see-through test. Even for an event after dark, don't get caught in something that shows more than you intended. For this, grab the camera again, a flashlight, and someone to help.

Indoors, preferably in front of a mirror, take the flashlight and point it at the front, back, and sides, as well as up and down. In natural daylight, take photographs from the front, back, and sides. Is anything too transparent?

Your friends might lie, but the camera never does.

good buy

For stylists, shopping isn't just shopping. It's market research. It's our job to know what products, stores, and labels are out there. The gig calls for being able to scrutinize the marketplace for the best resources.

To be your own stylist, strive to become a smart shopper. In the long run, it's going to save you money and streamline your closet. The aim is to love everything you own.

Buy something because you love it, you need it, and you *will* use it.

Begin by researching the market. This means shopping without actually buying anything. Know what's in your local stores, including those off the beaten track. There are so many great boutiques now, even in suburbia and in smaller neighborhoods, away from the major department stores and popular boutiques. Suss out who on the sales staff knows their stuff: they can prove to be great assets, calling you when new

Prep before the party

you love it, will use it.

merchandise arrives, telling you honestly whether something looks good or hideous, and revealing when something is going on sale. Having friends on the inside, so to speak, is a secret weapon for any stylist.

For stylists, finding the

right elements doesn't only require keeping your eyes wide open. It also helps to keep your options open, too, and the wider the better. Fashion now is so much about high and low dressing: pairing a $50 party dress from H&M with a pair of $400 Jimmy Choo heels. There are so many places to score gorgeous clothes and shoes at deliriously low prices. Take advantage of them, but be smart. Whether it's the mid-season sale at Net-A-Porter.com or eBay, the annual blowout at Barneys New York or the neighborhood resale shop, resist the urge to go bonkers just because something is at a slashed price.

Vintage is also a great way to go. Try curated vintage boutiques, thrift stores, or your great aunt's closet (where you might even score a gem for nothing). Avoid trendy for your red carpet look. Be realistic about what looks good on you—and what you will actually wear. Never buy something just because it's on sale. Always check the condition. And always check the return policy.

going vintage

*Among Hollywood red carpet regulars and international vintage collectors, Decades on Melrose Avenue in Los Angeles and its natty owner **Cameron Silver** top the list of resources for clothes, shoes, bags, and jewelry from the 1960s and 1970s (and sometimes earlier). Fashion houses worldwide not only rely on him to find great vintage for inspiration, but they also count on him to know what could be the next big trend. Come awards time, his shop is filled with A-listers and stylists looking for the kind of frock that will stand apart from what the other actresses are wearing—and send photographers into a tizzy.*

Here Cameron tells why vintage is the way to go for that special night. Plus he reveals his secrets to shopping for it.

"Who is this girl?" I wondered when I first met Rachel Zoe. She was visiting Los Angeles on a shoot. It's must've been 1988. Right there in Decades, we instantly bonded over our shared love for bold jeweled cuffs, Halston sheaths, and Hermès home accessories. When Rachel moved here, she became a great friend of mine and of the store's. Things come in all the time that I save for her. But sometimes she surprises me, like when she pulled a Rudi Gernreich swimsuit from the 1950s as a party look for one of her clients. Who knew?

What I do know is vintage, and there are few better resources to find a great party dress, let alone the jewelry and bag to go with it. Vintage is a very liberating option. If you buy it well, you're free from contemporary trends. It already went out of style once. If it withstood time, it's timeless! Just do your treasure hunting with eyes wide open and these ten tips in mind:

Vintage guru and Decades owner Cameron Silver

1 Ask yourself when you look at a vintage piece, does this look modern? That is the great irony: if something looks vintage, it might look costumey. But even an Edwardian piece can have a modern feel and work without looking like it's Halloween.

2 Condition is paramount. Look for armpit stains, moth holes, bead loss, and shattered hems. Certain blemishes can't be salvaged. There's only so much surgery you can do on a garment.

3 Beware of substandard fabrics. Disposable clothing from forty years ago is likely still disposable clothing today. Stick with quality fabrics.

4 Unless you're a hardcore collector, select vintage that you can wear, not archive. Buy clothes that have a little mystery, a little history.

5 Just because it's got a label doesn't mean it's good. A vintage piece has to have good design. It has to be wearable. For Lindsay Lohan's appearance at the opening of the Cartier flagship store on Rodeo Drive, Rachel chose a white Marilyn Monroelike halter dress by a relatively unknown American designer. The photographs ran like crazy.

6 Always go with your taste or that of someone you trust. People come to Decades because they trust our taste. They trust that we know good design and what's wearable.

7 Forget the trends, even in vintage. Your body really dictates what you can wear. Certain bodies look great in a 1950s dress, others in a 1970s sheath.

8 Vintage accessories can transform an outfit. You can wear the same little black dress over and over by changing your clutch.

9 With vintage jewelry, it's not about demure and safe. It's about statement. So, too, it doesn't have to be a huge investment or real.

10 Make it modern through the mix. Rachel does this very well, say, taking a 1950s dress and pairing it with some sexier, brightly colored Jimmy Choo heels and plenty of bling.

party prep

You receive an invitation. On it is the time, date, place, and even the reason for the celebration. What it doesn't list is the dress code. So what do you when the dress code is not on the invite? You find out. That's right. Don't ignore the matter altogether.

Always start with the cues right there on the invite.

CONSIDER THE VENUE

A prime cue is the location. An event held inside a grand ballroom might be formal, thereby demanding a more formal gown with a longer length. You may even be able to get away with a longer gown at a formal restaurant or a dinner at a home if the occasion calls for it, like a special anniversary or birthday.

In contrast, a party dress that skims the knee or above may be perfect for a special event held in a groovy downtown hole or a cocktail party at a friend's house. A garden party calls for a light option, cut from wispier fabrics and in looser silhouettes.

CONSIDER THE TIME

If it's Sunday at 4 P.M., chances are it's not a black-tie event. If it's a Saturday night wedding, say, after 6 P.M., it most certainly calls for a formal look.

A weekend brunch or an afternoon tea celebrating a birthday or baby shower calls for a little dress. Stay away from satin or other shiny fabrics for day. And resist black. I love black, but during the day, go with some other color. If you prefer darker shades, then try navy or brown or a deep jewel tone. But generally I prefer whites, creams, or even pastels for day.

If you're not in the mood for a dress, opt for a tailored jacket with a skirt or trousers, even if the style is relaxed. As a rule, these events are generally filled with women, so more feminine flourishes such as ruffles or florals are perfect.

Of course, a summer barbecue is bound to be a more casual affair. You don't want to get caught on the beach or on a lawn in stilettos, any more than you want to wear flip-flops to a cocktail party. Ditch the stilettos for wedges, which will keep you from sinking into the grass. Jeans are fine, but skip the scruffy T-shirt for a halter or poncho. If it's a pool party, do not forget a cover-up (be it a caftan or oversized scarf). No one really wants to see your bare booty—regardless of how fabulous it is—while they are digging into their dinner.

For these kinds of parties, I always grab another pair of shoes and a sweater and throw them into the trunk of my car. You don't want to leave a party that's just warming up just because the chills are getting in the way.

A CUE NOT TO BE OVERLOOKED: THE HOSTS

Who are they? If they tend toward dazzling, then you know that you, too, should go glam. If they're more casual, however, that doesn't give you license to go undone. You still want to respect your hosts. You can also always make a social call to them to find out what they're wearing. Then pass the message along to the rest of the party. It's good karma.

Stated dress code or not, there are times when throwing caution to the wind is perfectly right. I've always been a huge advocate of the maxim, "When in doubt, dress up." Even if it's just a notch up—a pair of gold strappy heels with skinny jeans—rarely will anyone question your decision.

Jennifer Garner in Valentino
at the 2004 Academy Awards

WHEN IN DOUBT . . .

If you show up looking a bit more glam than the rest, what's the worst-case scenario? You look the best in the room?

If someone gets catty over your decision, you can always just proclaim that you have another event to go to afterwards. Then it looks like you planned the night right—and that you have somewhere more fabulous to go! You can never really go wrong doing it up, as long as you feel—and act—comfortable.

Lindsay Lohan, who loves, loves fashion, can pull off a bit of overdressing at an awards show and come out looking more at ease than her fellow shabby-clad

and within yourself. Confidence doesn't come easy for everyone. I know. I'm in my mid-thirties, I dress women for a living, and I still have my ick days. But once you decide on something that you know looks amazing on you, do like Lindsay did, and own it. Don't allow yourself to become insecure. Don't make apologies.

Along those lines, don't wear something you're going to be fussing with during the party. If it requires constant retying, pulling, or adjusting, or it's something you're afraid is too transparent for comfort, then don't wear it. Do a self-check in the outfit before the event. You're there to have a good time, not to worry about your outfit.

If you show up looking a bit more glam than the rest, what's the worst-case scenario? You look the best in the room?

stars. Many of the bold-faced attendees who walked the red carpet of the 2006 Nickelodeon Kids' Choice Awards turned out in jeans and T-shirts. Yawn. Lindsay stood out in a bronzy ruffled minidress from Gucci. Although I was responsible for choosing the look off the recent fall runway show, I still warned her that she'd be more dressed up than the rest. Yet from her rose gold hoops to her gold heels, Miss Lindsay owned it. We kept her hair fresh with a ponytail, but we didn't demur when it came to the big bling ring. And you know, not one fashion critic jibed her for attending the awards show so dressed up. In fact, her photograph from that event continues to run as a hot pick.

Ultimately, whatever you choose to wear for a special event has to feel comfortable on the outside

A FOUNDATION TO BUILD ON

Beyond the spectacular couture, the pristine makeup and coifs, and the statuesque poses, the secret to looking amazing on the red carpet really does come down to what lies beneath. Pasties, cutlets, and slimmers and related secret weapons are very much a part of the artillery. I don't have a client who doesn't use them. Otherwise, it's all for naught if the world can make out your panty lines along with that gush where the waistline is cutting into your hip.

Choose underpinnings close to your skin color. If you still see panty lines under a dress, then drop the drawers and go nude. Get everything seamless. If budget allows, buy sets in white and black, too. But nude-colored basics are mandatory.

Determine what you're trying to conceal and reveal. Share these secrets with the salesperson when you're shopping for underpinnings. Need to slim your waist or thighs? Lift your bum? Take the time to find the right pieces.

When it comes to acquiring investment pieces for your wardrobe, the right bra, panties, and slimmers should top the list. Fill your drawers with pretty lace things in colors you would not even dare wear as a dress—but never at the expense of the basics. At the very least, every wardrobe should contain a selection of panties in full brief cut and, if you can manage it, ultra brief cut (such as a thong or string bikini). You need a bra that fits properly, so ask for the professional help of a salesperson at a lingerie department or shop. Seriously. It can change your life—not to mention your figure. A well-fitting bra is gold. This is one basic worth investing time and resources in.

In cases where a conventional bra gets in the way of the dress, try self-adhesive bras. They provide the support via sticky cups without the straps. To maximize cleavage apply them by keeping your arms close to the body.

As for keeping plunging necklines or skinny straps in place, toupee tape or any of the double-stick adhesive strips being marketed now for this use will keep you worry-free of a wardrobe malfunction. Adhesive for fake eyelashes also works great on spaghetti straps. Again, stand up straight when applying, then check yourself in the mirror before going out. If the sticky stuff is improperly applied, it will show and, just as badly, wrinkle the surrounding skin.

For my clients, I custom make or customize store-bought slimmers (what was once referred to as girdles) to fit under the length or parts of a gown and camouflage spots they don't think are so hot. Sometimes these beautiful, incredibly fit women don't even need it. But because it makes them *feel* more secure, it's worth it. If it's going to make you feel more confident, then wear it. There are so many types of slimmers at all kinds of price points now available.

Avoid short-length slimmers because they tend to create a line that can be seen through the dress, not to mention cut off circulation, which is not good for your legs or your health. If the dress is very short, wear opaque boy-cut panties or a silky tap pant. That way, if a wind should blow, you're okay.

You're there to have a good time, not to worry about your outfit.

dressed to kill doesn't mean overkill

Too much of anything is too much. Too much dress can distract from even the most beautiful face. Too much hair and makeup can age a woman. Too many visible designer logos cheapen your look.

THE NAKED TRUTH

So, too, when it comes to skin, never show too much of it. This might come as a surprise to some of you. I do love a backless sheath, or exposed shoulders. Mischa Barton looked divinely regal at the 2005 Golden Globes in a silver Azzaro that not only showed off her décolleté and shoulders, but also provided a peek at her hips and lower back because of a waist cutout. Months before, Rebecca Romijn wore a knee-length black silk charmeuse dress with a leg slit high up and a ruffled halter that plunged a bit.

But even among these earthly goddesses, I have my limits. It is not okay to walk into a formal or quasi-formal affair with an exposed midriff. Those days are long gone, thankfully. A rock-hard set of abs does not merit a free pass to show them to the world.

There are exceptions, of course, as there are to anything. Certain hot bods with recording contracts can get away with it if the event honors their industry, like the Grammys. Even then, I've tended to go with clothes that keep my clients' navels under wraps.

Among my personal all-time favorites is Kate Hudson at the 2003 Venice Film Festival. We went with a silver Chanel haute couture lace top and skirt that scarcely contained her five-months pregnant belly. The style was the height of chic at the time, but it was Kate's innate penchant for the boho luxe style

that made the choice effortlessly appropriate. But outside of Cher doing the same three decades earlier in Halston dresses that revealed her naked pregnant paunch, it is not a look for public consumption.

The same goes with rising hemlines, splits on a skirt, and plunging necklines. When it comes to too much leg or cleavage, there is an acceptable zone—for you and others. Otherwise it can get to a point where it makes others uncomfortable and turns a woman into a caricature. Think of that infamous 1958 image of Sophia Loren sneaking a peek at Jayne Mansfield's overtly exposed rack. The ever-sophisticated brunette, who had a grand set of her own, appears justifiably put off at Mansfield's naked ambition. Her look says it all.

Why detract from your mind, your face, your expression? The attention should be on *you*. Sexiness doesn't necessarily come with nakedness. I believe it's better to leave some things to the imagination, no matter how toned up a body is. If it's the opposite sex you're aiming to attract, believe me, any guy worth appealing to would rather wonder what it looks like under there than have you share it so magnanimously with the rest of the world.

STAND UP AND DRESS LIKE A WOMAN

Along those lines, microminis generally have no place at a special event. And in very few instances do microminis, paired with high boots or high heels, have a place anywhere once you're over twenty-four.

Blasphemous?

What's wrong with looking chic? Women need to be strong enough to say, "I don't need to dress like a teen girl any more." It's okay to be in sync with your young daughter or niece, but it's not okay to try to

look like her (whether it comes to clothes or plastic surgery).

There's something incredibly seductive about women who act like women.

Keep the glitz and glitter to nighttime. There are exceptions, of course. A bag, a sandal, and a top can have sparkling accents that work deliciously for daytime. You just don't want to be all blinged out while the sun is still shining. Full sparkle suggests a disco ball, so reserve the dance fever for after dark.

To wit: many showgirl flourishes that might look cute on teens and some twentysomethings look ridiculous beyond those ages. When I say glam, I don't mean in the Ziggy Stardust sense. Makeup with glitter in it? No. Feather boas? No. And as much as I love platform shoes, if they look like they belong on

members of the rock band KISS, a cartoony club kid, or a pole-dancing stripper, then definitely, unequivocally, no way.

And a reminder: sunglasses are not for nighttime. Even during the day, unless you're trying to create a moment from *Reservoir Dogs*, remove them when the camera points at you.

MASTER OF ILLUSION

If something is showing that you're not crazy about, *you will be uncomfortable.* Instead of obsessing over what you loathe about your body, focus on what you love—and show it off!

If you love your shoulders and arms, give them a public viewing. If you have great toned calves, flaunt

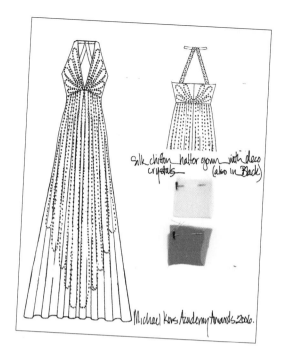

Silk chiffon halter gown with deco crystals (also in Black)

Michael Kors Academy Awards 2006.

them. Many of the most fuller-figured women I know won't wear a long dress because they want to show off their gams. And longer lengths can easily overpower a smaller woman. So a knee-length, even for formal affairs, may be a better alternative.

For curvy shapes, I love tailored pieces that showcase the figure. Choose clothes that nip at the waist and skim smoothly (not tightly) over the body. A little tummy is sexy, but if a slimmer doesn't do the trick, don't forgo a cinched waist altogether either. Go with flat-front trousers and side- or back-zip skirts that don't cling. If you don't want so much focus on a fuller bum, then opt for a fuller skirt and a closer-fitting top. Low-waist jeans or trousers deemphasize a generous backside (just don't go so low that you risk exposure).

If you want to deemphasize a voluptuous top half, wear something looser, like a blouse in a solid, dark color or minimal print. But keep the bottom half more fitted and in a lighter shade. Definitely avoid anything with prominent details on that zone of your body, including oversized lapels, chunky knits, wide-belt bucklers, or double-breasted anything.

While I don't think a flat figure needs to hide under a tent, go with a looser piece if it's more comfortable—but cinch the waist with a belt. A smaller-busted woman can get away with ruffles, embellishments, horizontal lines, and empire waists in particular. But don't be afraid of wearing fitted tops either. No need to hide what you have or bulk up.

For thicker or flabby arms, choose looks with a three-quarter sheer or opaque sleeve. Don't wear sleeves that cut into your arms, because they will only make your arms look bigger. Think of it as a game of smoke and mirrors. Except the aim is to look in the mirror and see a smokin' you. I'm a big advocate of accentuating the assets. But I stress accentuating—not distraction by way of overkill. In fact, it's a matter of assets and attitude. Some of the hottest women I know don't have model figures, but they sizzle because of their attitudes and actions.

Consider your body shape. Then find clothes that fit it—not the trends. Think proportions. Think dress code. And think what you can get away with that works best for you.

Black lace reembroidered Three tier gown with nude georgette lining and black silk satin trim.

Michael Kors Academy Awards 2006.

HAVING A FIT

Fit is everything. The way clothes fit can completely affect the way you feel. Think about how your favorite jeans can completely transform your mood. Clothes should never fit so tightly that they pucker or pull. They should skim a body enough to show off the shape—or at least play up the best parts. Remember, just because something's a fashion trend doesn't mean it's right for your body. Trying to force a look just because it's in fashion will only fail.

Just as importantly, a tailored fit can make or break an outfit. Something inexpensive can look vastly better once it has been tailored. And an incredibly expensive item can look horribly cheap if it fits terribly. Label or no label, if the fit is off, you do no justice to its maker and least of all to yourself. If you can't work a needle and thread, then go to your local dry-cleaner to have trousers hemmed or to get the sides of a dress cinched in. For less than ten bucks you can look like a million.

In the dressing room or during a fitting, don't forget to sit, walk, and check yourself out from all angles. Are the armholes too high or the shoulder edges extending beyond your frame? Does it play up your assets and camouflage your least favorite features?

Examine how the fabric lies across your chest and your hips. Whether vintage or new, the quality of the fabric and construction can make all the difference. Really examine it. Check out the stitching; test how the fabric responds when it's worn. A heavily textured boucle or brocade can add bulk, while a slinkier jersey or stretchy satin can reveal every lump and bump.

Stand up straight. Relax as you would if no one were looking. Be honest with yourself about how you appear in each pose. If you don't have a three-way mirror, turn slowly in front of the one you do have. Revealing, right? Yet the most revealing aid is photographs. Get someone to snap you from every angle.

inside the stylist's toolbox

Don't get dressed without these emergency fixers nearby:

- Toupee tape. This or a similar double-sided tape will keep in place a plunging neckline or errant strap. Hollywood Fashion Tape is a godsend.

- Eyelash glue. Use in cases when toupee tape is too wide, such as for spaghetti straps.

- Safety pins. In assorted sizes, but definitely have the tiny ones on hand.

- Broach. Jeweled or metal, keep one handy in the case of an instant nip and tuck.

- A small pair of scissors.

- A needle and thread. At a bare minimum, keep thread in black, white, light gray, and champagne on hand. Or consider the dominant colors in your wardrobe and stock up on those colors.

- Stain-removal sponges. There are several on the market now, including Miss Oops Rescue Sponges, which are especially amazing for erasing makeup and deodorant skidmarks from clothes.

- Tampons. Seriously. Stress can impact our bodies in all sorts of unexpected ways, and breakout periods have happened to too many of my clients. Shudder to think if you're not ready while wearing a white dress.

- Shoe insoles. Particularly helpful are nonslip triangles for high heels.

- Clear bandages. Blisters are not pretty. You don't want to be uncomfortable—or bleeding.

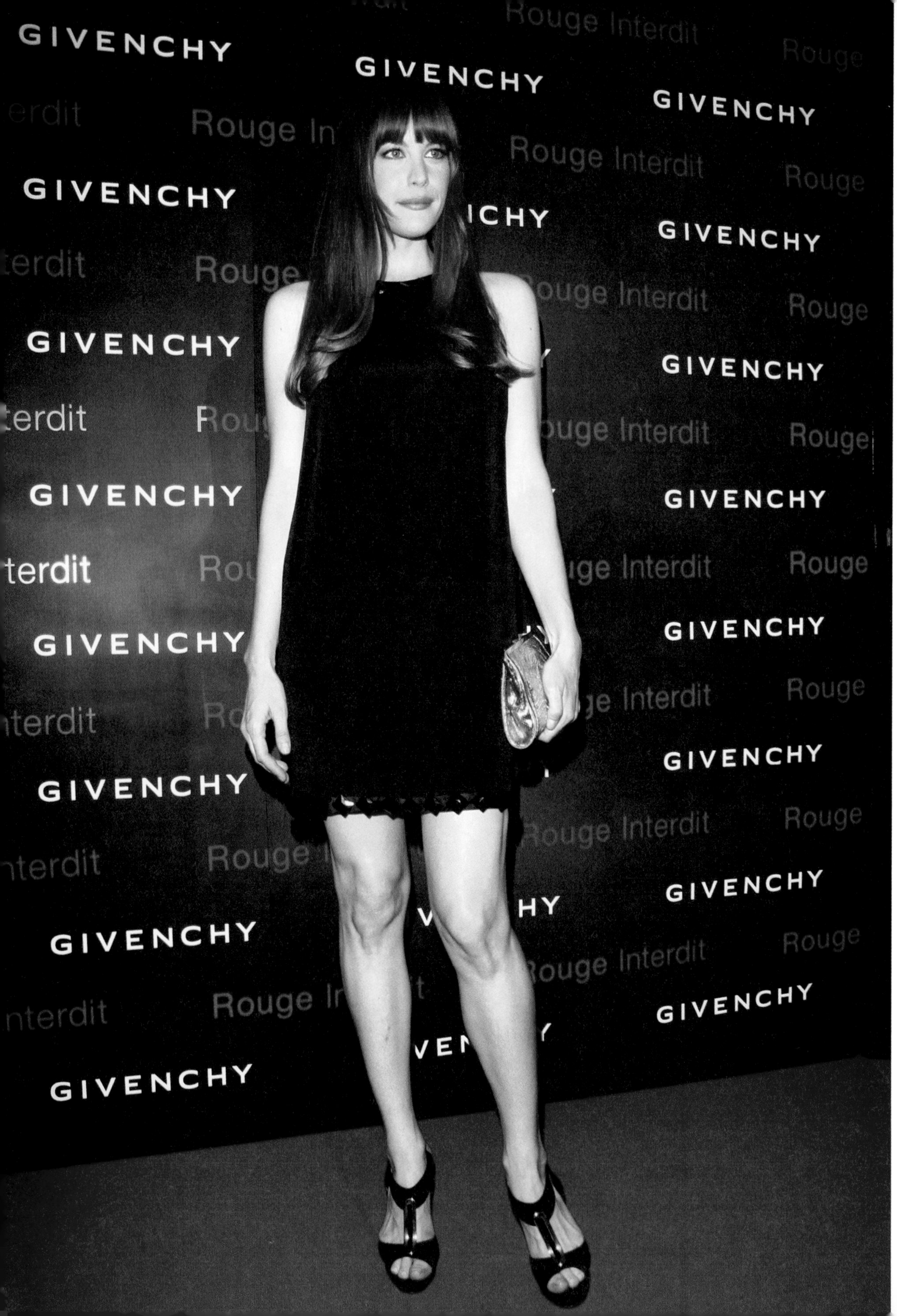
GIVENCHY
Rouge Interdit

cocktail parties

Gathering for cocktails should not simply be equated with alcohol. A cocktail party should be embraced as a marvelous excuse to dress up, even if it's just a little and even if the shindig is at home. A cocktail is a ritual of release, and so it should also be a bit of liberation from the professional uniform you wore all day.

THE LITTLE BLACK DRESS

The LBD is a perfect option for any cocktail party. If you can only own one, then choose a dress at or just below the knee, which is a chicer length than anything too mini and tarty or too long and frumpy. Resist a sexy neckline. A neckline that skims the cleavage is fine, but too plunging a V or scoop limits where you can wear it. So, too, anything that looks like a second skin. In most of life's situations, whether the occasion calls for dressing up or dressing down, opt for clothes with a bit of movement.

Choose a fabric that is versatile and wears well in countless scenarios. Unless you have the means for an unlimited number of LBDs, avoid wool, cashmere, and tweed, which only work in winter. Besides, these heavier fabrics tend to be quite thickening. The best fabrics to look for are chiffon, georgette, silk charmeuse, and tropical-weight wool jersey. If something more structured is in order, a silk or satin taffeta is really pretty, as is chiffon with corset-like seams or boning. I love a fabric that has a tiny bit of sheen to it.

WEARING THE PANTS

Sometimes the mood calls for pants. There's nothing sexier than being the sole woman clad in a tuxedo pantsuit at a gala filled with frothy frocks. When it comes to pants, stick to black, navy, white, and camel. Pinstripes are sexy in that Diane Keaton-Lauren Hutton kind of way.

A wide leg elongates the silhouette and can hide figure flaws. A higher waist also gives the illusion of a longer silhouette and flatters the waistline. I've always loved a high-waisted trouser.

But don't forget proportions. If trousers are loose, pair them with a tailored top. If pants are slim, go with a blouse, even if it's just blouson sleeves. Think Catherine Deneuve.

Liv Tyler in a Marchesa LBD at the Givenchy fragrance launch, Mexico City, 2007.

dinner parties

Dinner is the one meal when we can interrupt our wildly busy lives, come together, talk, and laugh. However informal, a dinner party deserves a change of clothes from what you wore running around all day. If you're invited to a dinner party be sure to call the hosts ahead and ask what they're wearing. Then spread the message.

GOING CASUAL

Unless the invite specifies a dress code or it's a holiday, go casual. But not all casual is executed equally. When I think casual, I think cozy—not sloppy.

A home is about feeling cozy. Suitable attire are jeans, a great top, and sexy shoes. Denim has come a long way, and if you know you'll feel more comfortable wearing jeans while sitting on the couch, enjoying a predinner glass of wine, then go with a pair in a clean silhouette and in a dark rinse. They look more streamline. Dress them up with a blouson or off-the-shoulder knit or poncho. Since even the coziest-looking homes can be drafty, always have a sweater on hand.

AT A RESTAURANT

If someone throws a dinner party at a restaurant, it's likely for a special reason. Even just bringing together old friends is reason enough. Dress up. Your host has spent resources and time on bringing everyone together. Besides, it's so much more fun when everyone dresses up. I love when guys wear a tie, or are at least primped up enough to complement the women guests. But don't go formal unless it calls for it, or it just might be the one time when overdoing it is really overdoing it! Size up the venue. If it's a burger joint, casual is fine. But even then, wearing a little dress can be right.

Dressing for dinner is one tradition we've unfortunately let go by the wayside. What's amazing in Europe is how even in small towns everyone still gets dressed up for dinner. In America, we've come to the point—and not just in L.A.—where guests show up to the most posh restaurants wearing scraggly jeans. When people underdress they actually bring a lot of attention to themselves. Dressed up, you can't help but feel great.

I say, let's bring back that sense of dressing up.

Keira does tea-length vintage Ossie Clark to the Oscar nominee luncheon, 2006.

light of the party: alberta ferretti

Sometimes a special event doesn't call for a ball gown. But it does necessitate something special, even pretty, and pretty doesn't have to mean sweet, or even old-fashioned. Delicate fabrics come off with strong sophistication in the able hands of Italian designer Alberta Ferretti, and my clients and I adore her for it. Four decades into realizing her ideas in cloth, Alberta knows dresses better than most.

While a long gown may be required for a theater premiere or event where formal dress is expressly requested, it can be an unnecessary overdressed effect for, say, an art opening. Yet, life has become so fast-paced that to keep up, we have become even more informal.

Fortunately, "dressing up" has become de rigueur again among women and men. But the key is to avoid the all-too-routine *"escamotage de la petit robe noir"*—that is, escaping into the safe little black dress. Instead, consider a dress made

of more precious fabrics such as silk gazar or chiffon, as in an ethereal dress with a voluminous skirt and cinched with a beautiful belt—an elegant silhouette. For a summer or pool party, a short evening dress or a caftan looks great. Freshness and lightness are two important elements.

The most modern way to dress—for parties *and* everyday life—is by respecting your own personality and proportion. You will feel more comfortable and at ease. Rachel has this sense of modernity where she knows to consider her client's personality and body type for every occasion. When she uses my dresses, she chooses with an intimate knowledge of what will really work. Her choices are never "too much," but still very elegant.

It is only when personality and proportion are regarded that a woman's natural glamour is enhanced by the dress. You can and should be elegant at every age. Femininity is an adjective that stands apart from the dress and the age. It is a concept that never goes out in my fashion—not with my signature collection or the Philosophy line, two different brands that are able to reveal a woman's potential at any age.

It's a mistake to think of a dress as a costume. Too many times, women think they are attending a masked ball instead of a party, and they dress up as a character that doesn't reflect their personality. More often than not, it is out of insecurity—believing the overtly sexy, as in aggressive cleavages and slits, will get them more attention. To me, the biggest gaffe is dressing up for others and not for ourselves.

'TIS THE SEASON

Holidays are the perfect time to bring out all those party dresses and gorgeous accessories you bought throughout the year, including the ones hiding in your closet with the tags still on.

At holiday time you're expected to dress up. There certainly are exceptions, like when the host indicates it's a tree-lighting party with pizza. But even then, I've walked into clients' homes and found them in pajamas to light up the tree while I was in a fur. No matter. 'Tis the season, and I love to chill out on the floor with the kids no matter how glam I turn out. I think holiday time is the perfect excuse to dress up (as if I need an excuse). Haul out the pieces cut from heavier, richer fabrics: velvet, fur, brocades, and duchess satin. There's no better time for metallics, paillettes, beads, and crystals. Even if you go with jeans, punch up the look.

Crucial to remember: Plan out the season. When it comes to red carpet moments among my clients, I always advise them to remember the audience. No one wants to get caught in photographs in the same look at more than one event, and you may have more than one party in a matter of weeks. With that in mind, it takes a little strategizing—even if you don't have a different look for each party.

Mark your calendar. Ponder the guest list as best as you can. Then think through your outfits. If you have to recycle a dress for more than one event, try not to wear it among the same "audience," and accessorize it differently each time. Nor do you want to waste the season's best dress in your wardrobe at a so-so event. Planning prevents such mishaps. It particularly avoids the end of the season shocker: reviewing your photographs from a handful of parties and realizing that you look the same at most of them!

Even a shorter length can convey maximum glamour, especially when it comes speckled in sparkle like this Dior.

There's no better time for metallics, paillettes, beads, and crystals.

red carpet

Of the endless facets to my job, the red carpet remains one of my favorite tasks. For me, it's like being a parent and seeing my grown child off to the prom. After a dozen-plus years doing this, I still get a huge rush. The red carpet is obviously a showcase for what I do, but more importantly, it's an opportunity for a celebrity to present another side of herself. Who doesn't like to do that?

LOOKING GOOD IS NOT ALWAYS FEELING IT

There will be times when getting gorgeous may have to override comfort.

For a dinner I co-hosted with Francisco Costa, I wore a corseted gown of his design. It was black lace and beautiful. Some women love the structure of a corset—my clients who are prepared to suffer for fashion will suck it up for the sake of an evening.

Me? I don't even like to wear bras. I wear jersey and drapey shapes. I prefer a relaxed glamour. In Francisco's dress—although it fit beautifully because it was tailored for me—I was uncomfortable inside. Of course, for the love of fashion and friendship with the designers, I sometimes suck it up, too.

In other cases, certain hairstyles or trendier gowns might seem like a good idea at the time. We've all been there. Certain choices I made in high school definitely haunt me now. But I've since learned to always ask myself if I'm going to be happy through the evening or fretting all night. Will I look back in ten, twenty years and still love this look?

Finding your red carpet gown isn't that different from the hunt for other party looks. Be realistic. Avoid trendy. Buy a gown from a store where it's returnable. You may change your mind in a month, and that impulse purchase you made for fear that it might be gone if you don't buy it now isn't always a wise one.

Prepping in advance allows you to experiment with makeup, hair, the underpinnings. Walk around the house in those new shoes. Snap those pre- photos. It pays to be a little neurotic in advance. But don't be afraid of a little risk. These moments exist so we can realize our wildest dreams.

how to shine *at the big event?*

Francisco Costa, the handsome Brazilian who is reinvigorating Calvin Klein as its creative director, is always coming up with new and modern ways for women, some incredibly famous, to dress for the many special events in their lives, from personal parties to award shows. Here he shares his insight on red carpet dressing, even if it's dressing for your own "red carpet" moment.

It's important to keep it simple. I'm not a big fan of anything too fussy on the back of a dress. It's all good and well to make a dramatic exit. But is it realistic? You want others to see you head on, to experience your smile and personality. At awards shows, when an actress wears a dress with all the focus on the back, she's more concerned with showing it to the cameras than with just standing there and enjoying herself. Where's the fun in that?

Of course, a dramatic feature has its place. Amazing shoulders unveiled, a waist that is accentuated, or a fabulous leg revealed from a high split in the dress. Even a very open, low back.

The best dresses frame the figure and the face, emphasizing the best features. A tailor is so important. You could be wearing a dress that costs nothing but no one will notice if it fits perfectly. So, too, when it comes to shoes and nails. Skimp on the dress if you must, but not the shoes. Get a manicure.

The women who look most beautiful—and are most successful at it—are those who appear to be floating through the room because they are so at ease in what they're wearing. They can work the room because they aren't weighed down by their dresses. They're dancing. They may have opted for flat sandals instead of heels like everyone else. And all the while the princesses in their stiff, overwhelming taffeta gowns are sitting there watching.

At black-tie events of any occasion, some women tend to overdo it. Too much hair. Too many jewels. No one is really at ease when they require security guards. There's nothing modern in that.

Who can resist a man in a tux? The irresistible Francisco Costa on the night of his Council of Fashion Designers of America win, 2006.

Ultimately, whatever amazing dress you wear, what makes it a great red carpet choice is that you feel and look natural in it. This is a very American attitude, rooted in a tradition of effortlessness in sportswear. Look at Rachel. She might be in a fur, but she has a very sportswear sensibility to her style even when she's all dressed up.

men in black tie

*Among the new style setters, few men—or women—can compete with the ever–dapper designer **Zac Posen**. He can work a tuxedo like a second skin. So I'll let him tell you guys how to rock it right.*

Why should a guy concern himself with how he dresses? For his own amusement, of course. I enjoy dressing up. Personally, I draw inspiration by linking the avant-garde with the chic conservative. There's so much frivolity in men's dress historically. So in these times of high casualness, it's good for all men to dress up. It's vital for straight men to catch the eye of a lady.

I don't believe in the chic banal. Risk taking in dress is very important. That means mixing high luxury classics like Turnball & Asser with the more forward Dior Homme. Mixing black and navy. Or go with a Chinoiserie smoking jacket, like those found in vintage stores. Or an opera cape!

I take every opportunity to don a tuxedo. I have so many, some forty-five and counting. Let's start with the lapels of the tuxedo. Satin lapels are only for fall through winter. Grosgrain or faille is best for fall. For spring to summer, go with self-finished self lapels. Wide lapels are romantic, but on most guys they can look goofy. And the notch of the lapel should always be high, a visual device that can balance a lot of men's poor posture. A single-button, shawl-collar jacket is always soft and elegant. Men above 5-foot-9 can get away with double-breasted jackets; men below that height are better off sticking to a nondouble-breasted shorter jacket. If there's more than a single button on the jacket, wear only one of them—the center one—buttoned. Never completely button up a tuxedo or any suit.

I'm a big believer in cummerbunds. It lends a bit of security while providing a beautiful elegance, an international sophistication, to a look. It should always be faille, not satin. Pleats up, never down. Only don a vest if you're slim—it's not a girdle; otherwise go with a cummerbund.

I like a real bow tie. If you can't tie it, have it tied in advance and sew it in place so that it never comes undone. A great way to go is to wear a white faille bow tie with a shawl collar (though if you do it with a double-breasted look, you'll end up looking like a waiter). A pink bow tie is a great option, too. When the dress code calls for black tie, it's also possible to go with a necktie worn with a loose knot, like a half cravat, tucked into the shirt.

Dress shirts look best with a French cuff. After all, cuff links are a great talking point for women. On a budget? Enamel cuff links are beautiful. If you don't have cufflinks and are in a bind, simply take the extra sleeve buttons from the jacket and sew them back-to-back. I love a pleated shirt, or one with a standing collar with the points. But never do too wide a collar. The skinnier the collar is, the longer your neck looks.

It's very polite to always have a handkerchief. Fold it into a four-point napkin. Here's an opportunity, as with the cuff links, to be more frivolous with pattern or color, matching the bow tie and hankie. Satin is okay if it's a black shirt with a black tux. But nothing beats a nice white linen napkin with a white shirt. This is also a great place for a hidden gesture like a monogram.

Insofar as the pants, I'm not a fan of partial-front pleats. They come off looking too penguin. A full pleat down the leg or a clean flat front is a great way to go. A cuff is also fantastic. The side stripe should be a clean satin or faille. A break in a pant leg is most important. A skinny leg is fine for jeans, but for evening, a wider leg, even a bootleg, is more attractive on a man. See your tailor.

The chicest thing in the world is a man in dress slippers—black patent or velvet—with a tuxedo. Something very Gaucho Club, very louche. Just don't forget to score the bottoms or you'll inevitably slip on some marble floor. Don't overlook the hosiery either. Slip on a thin silk sock in papal pink, dusty cypress green, or black or white. Lastly, there are the extras that are in no way superfluous. Keep keys and wallet to a minimum. Just go out with what you will really need. Leather gloves are nice. A watch is important. Tie pins are fantastic, as are matching sets of shirt studs and cuff links. They're all a great way to inject an accent of color. I love turquoise on white, or matte Aztec gold.

Jewelry has to be very masculine and not too highly decorative, although I have worn a long strand of pearls to great effect: underneath the jacket and just peeking out a bit. Very Coco. A very small corsage, especially a carnation in two-tone or purple, is very chic. A single tuberose with a long stem or, in winter, a sprig of a yew tree or pine is also nice. Put them through the buttonhole instead of pinning them flat.

Don't forget a thin pen, slipped into an inside pocket. A man should always carry a pen. I love to in case I want to sketch something. But it's also imperative for jotting down an important phone number. Leave the PDA at home! Making it part of your black-tie ensemble is terribly uncouth.

To the hilt dressed in gold Donna Karan and with my dear Zac Posen in Manhattan

chapter 3
the day after

there is life after the party, of course. It might not have as much sparkle, but it's just as essential to look good— and look the part when it comes to career and casual time.

Don't believe for a moment I subscribe to any notion that dressing for work or play means dull. Or even subdued, for that matter. Glamour has its place in these arenas of life, too. It just doesn't have to come in high-octane form. It can show up as a simple accessory or other flourish appropriate to the *affairs du jour*. But when it comes to the office, think chic instead of glitz. When it comes to a day off, go effortlessly haute instead of lazily scruffy.

clocking in

My work uniform, generally, is a pair of black jersey pants or dark washed jeans, a drapey shirt, and either a little jacket, a fur vest, or a knit wrap. Going into spring, one of my favorite looks is a flowing jersey dress with wedges, and maybe a belt. I'm always on the move, so I need to be comfortable and not feel constricted. For winter, I throw on a drapey knit sweater, a wrap, or a jacket over leggings. Turtlenecks look great on some people, but not me (claustrophobia!). I prefer a cowl-neck sweater.

No matter the season, I base my outfit around my jacket. A jacket (or vest or wrap) can give any outfit a finished effect. It guards against unexpected chill inside or outdoors. I also usually tuck my jeans into some sort of boot, and trade from a pile of chains, cuffs, and oversized earrings. I can do that in an unconventional field like styling celebrities. But my field is not corporate America.

CORPORATE IDENTITY

Just as there are standards for dressing for the red carpet or a cocktail soiree, there are codes within every industry and profession that shouldn't be seen as restrictions, but as opportunities to let you—and not just your clothes—grab the attention.

Generally, the workplace is no place for too much skin. Plunging necklines and exposed backs can look right at a dinner with friends but come off as horribly cheap looking in the office, no matter how much you doled out for the top. Microminis? Forget it. Same for midriffs. Unless you're actually employed in a nightclub, your workplace is no place to dress like you're at one.

If a top is riding up or jeans drop so low that skin peeks out, choose a separate that provides coverage without constant tucking or tugging. Layering a longer T-shirt or blouse under a shrunken top or sweater is one solution.

Don't leave the house without pairing a sheer blouse with a camisole or tank top. Do the same if a top is cut very low in the front. Layering can actually polish a look. Or try wrapping an oversized scarf around the neckline. Cleavage is not an option at the workplace. And no matter how cute the bra, keep straying straps in place by tightening them or using double-stick tape, just as you would with a dressed-up look.

The barometer should be your own common sense. If you're at all conscious an outfit is showcasing too much of your boobs or your thighs, then it probably is.

None of this means, you have to dress like a man. The corporate codes that resulted in linebacker-sized shoulder pads in the 1940s and again in the 1980s—both decades when women markedly rose in the professional ranks—are out. Even if your office dress code requires business attire, you can look amazing and appropriate in pencil skirts, tailored jackets, button-down shirts, and even a blouson with a ruffled neckline.

In a corporate environment, think suit dressing—even if you don't wear matching pants. Throw the jacket from a suit over a tailored, knee-length shift or a wraparound dress. Work a cardigan with an A-line skirt or trousers. A vest or short-sleeved sweater, either in a fine cotton or cozy cashmere, worn over a blouse or button-up shirt suggests suit.

Of course, nothing evokes a sense of power like an actual suit. A beautifully cut suit in a neutral, seasonless fabric (such as tropical wool or gabardine) can be a stress-free uniform—and the best investment you can make in your wardrobe. Go with a silhouette that is clean and classic. You can give it a hit of personality, and color, by way of a necklace or broach or a colored blouse or turtleneck. Just

Unless you work at a fashion magazine or a stripper bar, stay away from five-inch platforms.

keep it elegant and to the point. Belts, skinny or wide and cinched at the waist or hips, provide another great finishing touch. Shoes shouldn't be too distracting. Keep anything too embellished, metallic, or high in your bag for after work. Sensible doesn't have to be conservative, but it should be tasteful and suitable, as in a beautiful leather stiletto pump or wedge instead of a funky platform. So, too, your bag. Nothing too cute or fussy. You're going to the office, not a party, so do yourself and your look a favor and go with a shoulder bag or tote that can hold everything you need for work—a laptop, a PDA, files . . . *and* your happy-hour heels.

Even in a more casual or creative milieu, where jeans are perfectly appropriate, top them off with a blouse and maybe a jacket. The jeans should be a bit dressier—no holes, no faded spots, no ratty edges. There's no need to become a fashion casualty just because it's Casual Friday.

Rebecca Romijn rocks an otherwise prim suit with the highest of heels and a fabulous smile.

diane von furstenberg

*If anyone knows how to work the workplace in the chicest terms it's **Diane von Furstenberg**. In the midst of a second coming as the head of a prosperous and thriving international empire that bears her name, DVF continues to represent modernness, drive, grace, and glamour. Her signature style makes her as much a relevant force today as ever. Don't even think of clocking in at the office without taking in some of her career advise.*

Even on her day off Diane von Furstenberg is the epitome of glamour.

You don't have to look like a man. Those days of dressing masculine in order to be taken seriously are over. Look like a woman. It's a person's confidence that speaks volumes, from a presentation to a sales call. And few things are more stylish, bring out beauty, than confidence.

Of course, confidence comes from being comfortable in who you are. Do not try to be somebody else. Find your own way in the clothing and hair you feel truly most you in, most comfortable. That will bring about confidence.

Obviously you want to look neat. But avoid anything too forced, whether it's hair, or makeup, or clothes that don't move. Certainly, the wrap dress is a perfect uniform, but so is a skirt or trousers. You have to look at your environment, the purpose of your day, and how you want to project yourself. You wouldn't dress the same to ask for a raise as you would if you were going to meet your boyfriend. But really, going to the office is like going to church. A skirt that is too mini is not right. Chewing gum should be banned. It's so unattractive. You should have respect for your employer, your co-workers, and, most of all, yourself.

I love jewelry. Accessories are a punctuation of your personality, and I never, ever go out without my huge gold bracelet. But your choices should not get in the way or be distracting. Find a utilitarian tote that looks good and can contain your entire world. You don't want to be caught without something needed to get a job done. As for your heel height, it doesn't matter as long as you feel steady and solid on your feet, whatever the long day demands.

Take into consideration that a boot or skirt or suit influences the way you walk and sit, your attitude. It can determine the kind of day you have as you deal with a boss or a crisis. Overall, enjoy being the woman you are. To do that, exercise a little, eat properly. Don't look like a slob. It's all about being your own best friend, respecting and liking who you are.

Or flip the template: pair trousers with a T-shirt. Skinny or wide-leg, nothing beats a great pair of well-fitting trousers in solid or pinstripe. Consider proportion: looser trousers and a closer-fitting T-shirt; slim legs and a blousy top. A pairing that is all too tight or all too loose can wind up appearing too sexy or too messy.

Unless you're a lifeguard, don't do flip-flops. A dressier shoe, flat or with a heel, can qualify jeans for most workplaces.

By playing it half casual, half tailored, your overall look comes off less buttoned-up but still professional. Casual isn't carte blanche for sloth. You still want to project that you're on your game.

The workplace is also no place to be too glam. I did say *too* glam. Instead, go with a mannerism or a quiet flourish of an accessory (say, gold chains and small gold hoops). Save anything that is too metallic, too sparkling, and too showy for after hours. Diamond or crystal studs are on the mark, but chandelier sparklers or shoulder-grazing hoops are too much. Unless you work at a fashion magazine or a stripper bar, stay away from five-inch platforms. In a workplace, heel height should max out at three inches. Being chic should always be the goal.

As a rule, resist anything extreme—too much hair, too much glitz, and too much skin. Sticking to a neutral palette, too, such as black, browns, and whites, intimates a sense of subtle elegance.

Remember, just because something's a trend doesn't mean it belongs in an office. Your workplace might be casual, but ripped jeans or flip-flops should be reserved for slumming on a Saturday. Casual clothes typically encourage casual manners. Even as dress codes become more relaxed and fashion trends at times veer into unrealistic zones, the goal at work should always be the same: to make a statement based on your brilliance and abilities—not on your body or clothes.

How to manage a look that's both relaxed and professional looking? Zac Posen pulls it off to perfection in a crisp white T-shirt, trim chinos, and jewelry or (as in my case) a dressier jacket over tailored trousers.

day off

Your day off should be about comfort, but again, comfort doesn't equal sloppy. A day off from work or from other formal situations doesn't have to mean a day off from style.

I'm the biggest champion of being comfortable in clothes, and I don't just mean psychologically. Comfort has to come physically, too, which is why I live mostly in jersey and cashmere. But somewhere along the line, in our casualization of dress codes, the message has gotten

Casual can mean tailored. Go with clothes that fit your figure and accessories that pull it all together, like this wide belt.

totally twisted. Rich or poor, famous or not, too much of the world seems to think it's perfectly acceptable, even cool, to look rumpled and raggedy. Even worse, there's a prevailing misconception that it's somehow easier than looking sharp. A big yawn to that. I mean, where's the imagination, the self-regard in looking like that? Where is the joie de vivre!

Earth shattering as this may sound, tracksuits—no matter how cute, fuzzy, or sexy—are for lounging at home or working out. Leave sweat suits, including faded drawstring pants, battered T-shirts, and your favorite old oversized hoodie, for the gym, *please*. Don't even get me started on baseball caps. Outside of the ballpark, could there be anything more tired?

The aim on your day off is to look effortlessly smart. Consider an outfit that in any given scenario you might come across, or with any special someone you might meet, you won't feel embarrassed or constricted. You do, after all, want to feel completely at ease. But avoid any look that

suggests you just rolled out of bed. It's simple. A belted, oversized cardigan, vintage or new, with a pretty top (even a well-fitting T-shirt) is great over your weekend jeans or leggings.

Dresses are another ideal option. I love a dress that can just be thrown on and moves every which way yet stills look perfectly put together. A classic Diane von Furstenberg wrap dress or a convertible Norma Kamali boatneck dress (both of which come in jersey and look right in most offices) can be sexy or straightforward depending on the belt and shoes. And you can still sit cross-legged on the floor or dance the light fantastic in them, should the moment or muse arise.

When going casual, choose clothes made of fabrics that merge comfort and a little luxury—jersey, cashmere, cotton. Choose fluid shapes, such as off-the-shoulder tops and loose pants. Just beware of anything too roomy, as it might resemble a muumuu. Turn up the style on a tank top and pair of jeans with a great cotton or cashmere wrap and boots or flats (instead of sneakers). A printed head scarf or pulled back, ever-so-slightly mussed-up hair can finish the look.

Your luxe but casual wardrobe doesn't have to max out the plastic. Shop for separates, dresses, and accessories that embrace both laid-back comfort and high style, and you can look like you're living it up even on your days off.

A sweater dress, like this striped Stella McCartney turtleneck on Cameron Diaz, instantly provides a finished appearance at the job or on a day off . . .

...as does this fluid jersey Calvin Klein sheath on Joy Bryant.

chilling with molly sims

A day off is no excuse to be a slob. I won't do the cropped tank top, jeans, and Ugg boots look. No one wants to see your belly button at the Coffee Bean. My New Year's resolution last year was not to leave luxury or the nice things in my closet for special occasions, but to enjoy them even on the days I'm slumming it.

Molly Sims on her day away from official biz

I might work fourteen hours on the set, undergoing hair, makeup, and several costume changes. But the next day, when I can go casual and with little or no makeup, I still like to look finished. That's what I love about Rachel. Even dressed down, she has style. I strive for that, too, even if it's just jeans and a cool T-shirt.

My days off usually involve running errands, yoga, and lunch with girlfriends. In fact, they're really not totally "off," as I always have so much to do. Because of that, I never know what I'm going to end up doing or who I'll end up running into—all the more reason not to look like a mess.

I usually wear jeans or a simple dress I can throw on. I love leggings, too, with either short dresses or a long white shirt with a belt. The goal is comfort, so I always wear cardigans or oversized sweaters.

I'm tall, so I typically wear flats to run around in. There are so many great styles—patent, gold, ballerina. I can't get enough, especially since I've never been a sneaker kind of girl. Still, there are a lot of cool styles out there now, and I love my Converse slip-ons without the laces.

I may get a call to spontaneously meet someone for drinks, so I always try to keep a couple of cool pieces in the car—a cute jacket and heels. I'm usually already in something I could wear into night with just a change of shoes, and maybe earrings.

The bag, too, can change the look. During my days off, the one piece I always have is an oversized bag to carry everything I need for the day—makeup, hairbrush, iPod, a book or script. I always carry something I can read while I'm waiting in a line. I also throw in a smaller purse—usually a clutch in natural leather that goes with anything—in case I want to run into dinner without hauling this big bag.

I get away without doing my hair or wearing too much makeup by using a scarf or headband and big sunglasses. The look is easy and fabulous, a throwback to Grace Kelly.

denim rules

I believe jeans can be worn in a mile-long list of scenarios. I wear them for work and play, of course, and occasionally on a night out celebrating. I also believe denim should be used, and not abused.

These days people are a little too cozy with the notion that all denim is for all things. Not so. Never underestimate the power of denim, including when it doesn't fit the situation. Jeans can be sexy for a date. They're ideal for running around on your day off or for a dinner party at a best friend's house. Some jeans could even be right for work—depending on the office's dress code and culture. But when it comes to a company event, unless it's some hoedown barbecue, opt for a little more than denim out of respect for your employers and industry. A dress or pair of trousers is no more difficult to get into or less relaxed, and it makes an entirely better statement. No matter how much you glam jeans up, they are still jeans.

For all other times, especially a party or date, dress denim up. Throw on a pair of notice-me heels or flashy flats and a jacket. A belt, even if it's a rolled-up scarf, looped and knotted at the side or front, can bump a look up a notch without much effort.

Keep in mind that when it comes to denim there are very, very different rules for civilians and supermodels. A glamazonian accident of nature (because, let's face it, that what they are, in the best way, of course) can make even low-rise, acid-washed pedal pusher jeans look like a good idea. For the rest of us, finding the best silhouette for our bodies—and not the trendiest denim incarnation—is the way to go. Keep it basic. Studs, embroidery, and other embellishments can certainly provide some interest, although not always to great effect. First think of jeans as a base to build on. Having at least one pair (or more) of great fitting, go-to jeans is a crucial element in a wardrobe.

Maria Sharapova works stovepipe jeans in a dark rinse accessorized with great jewelry and heels.

FINDING YOUR BEST SILHOUETTE

Let's get one truth immediately out of the way: there is no finger-snap shortcut to finding the perfect pair of jeans. Even within a brand, five different styles can fit five different ways. When the search begins for those go-to jeans, be prepared to shimmy into as many pairs as it takes until you reach the magical pair that makes you feel and look your most confident and most fabulous. No matter the time or the number of jeans or stores, make the effort. It's worth it.

Rises have dropped to incredible levels in recent years, but only a very tiny segment of the population should be wearing extremely low-rise jeans. And the number among us who can get away with the average low-rise jeans is not much higher.

Unfortunately, the masses have not quite grasped this concept in their eagerness to jump on and into this trend. The result is not pretty, with too much tush cleavage and flesh rolls pouring over the waistline now the norm.

Great-fitting, great-looking jeans should not look like they're squeezing you out like sausage from its casing. If the waist cuts into your hips or any other line of your torso, creating a fat roll, cast those jeans off immediately! In all likelihood, you don't need to diet (which is what you would tell yourself every time you pull them on). You just need a different silhouette and size.

The leg should flatter your shape. A skinny tapered leg is great yet typically not the best option on pear-shaped bums. If that's your figure and you love the look of super-skinny jeans, pair them with a shirt or top that extends just beyond your thighs. On shorter gams, the hem should skim the floor to give the illusion of longer legs. A long length, in fact, looks great on all heights of people, but the scraggly, dirty hems that have become so prevalent are not attractive.

I love a high-waisted jean on long legs. If your legs are super thin or you're self-conscious about any part of them (calves, thighs), wear a high-waisted, full-cut trouser jean. There are so many great versions out there.

It's important to keep in mind that what works on your friend may be all wrong for you. Always consider your own body type when it comes to getting into a pair.

In all likelihood, you don't need to diet.
You just need a different silhouette and size.

anne hathaway *cracks the jean code*

When I was a teen in the mid-1990s, jeans were not the fashion statement they are now. I wore loose-fitting, high-waisted, shapeless basics. Now jeans have become a status symbol, a luxury item. They even require a little education about them—but don't be intimidated. Jeans are still about comfort and earthiness. They are also very sexy, and very much about fashion. Jeans are cut so well now, and they are available in such a great assortment of fabrics—cashmere, wool blends, you name it.

I live in jeans. My daily uniform is either a casual dress or jeans. I prefer outfits that look like I cared but don't come off as too dolled up. Jeans serve as a great base for showcasing a pretty top and great accessories. A well-fitting dark pair can be dressed up for dinner, even a last-minute meeting. All the while, they feel perfectly comfortable.

If you're thin you can probably get away with a stiff jean. If you're like me, and a bit curvy, then some stretch is the way to go. There are even some brands that manage to cut a skinny jean with stretch that looks good on the rest of us shapely girls.

When you go shopping for jeans (or anything else) be kind to yourself. If a pair of jeans doesn't fit, don't take it as a personal failure. Shrug it off, throw the jeans aside, and move on. It might take some patience, but you will find the perfect pair. Bring a friend and a camera along. When you pose for the camera in the dressing area, don't do it straight on. Be real. Cock your hip and stand as you would in the real world. Never buy jeans that are too small with the idea that someday you'll squeeze into them. Live in the present. And be open to more than one brand. The fit can vary among brands and styles, and even from year to year.

When you finally find jeans that flatter your figure, buy two pairs: one to wear with heels, the other with flat shoes. If your budget doesn't allow for two, then get double-sided tape. Nothing is worse than frayed, dragging bottoms. It takes less than ten minutes to fold the cuff under, iron it flat, and tape it in place.

Perfect-fitting jeans can also replace your bathroom scale. Go with jeans that fit your healthy body weight. I know I have to skip dessert or order a second according to whether my favorite pair is too tight or loose. A darker rinse (or even black) tends to be more flattering, because faded features attract light in all the wrong places, especially in photographs.

My favorite way to dress jeans up? Paired with a tailored cardigan or a pullover sweater, a great blazer, and high boots—always high. I don't like mid-height. I either do ballet flats or five inches. Dressing jeans up with a sky-high heel elongates the

Keira Knightley

TOO BLUE

There is such a thing as too much of a good thing. Head-to-toe denim is one of them, and a huge lapse of judgment. I get hives just thinking about it. Unless you're a cowboy, a denim "outfit" demands to be broken up. Go with the jeans or go with the jacket, but never go with both at the same time.

As for colored denim? White jeans are so chic. Black or gray suggests an edgy elegance, particularly in the right cut (skinny stove pipes do the trick, hands down). But the rainbow of hues that comes into fad every few years looks good on very few, usually among those who didn't live it the first go-round, including those wear-anything supermodels who were too young to have worn red, yellow, and turquoise jeans the last time they were on trend. My advice: stay away from colored denim.

If you can, keep one pair of jeans in a deep dark rinse and another lighter pair. Also, it's good to have one pair in the closet that fits looser than the other.

CARE

Great jeans are hard enough to find, so when I do finally score my favorite blues, I want to preserve them. I dry-clean jeans to keep them crisp and dark for as long as possible. If drycleaning seems extravagant, you can wash them in cold water and hang them out to dry.

day-off footwear

Those who know me know I *live* in heels. On my day off, my flip-flops are canvas platform espadrilles.

At fifteen I refused to wear flats or sneakers. I had this fantastic pair of sandals with black wood wedge heels that I loved so much. I strapped them on as much as possible. Even up a mountain I had to conquer. And, no, I don't mean some metaphorical tale of reaching my goals. It really was a mountain in Grand Teton, Wyoming.

The hike was part of a summer camp that every good Jewish girl in my circle participated in as some kind of rite of passage into womanhood. *Please*. Those platforms, the royal blue eyeliner, and tall cans of hair spray to keep my oversized 'do in place were my rites of growing up. On that hike I wore a denim miniskirt, a *Flashdance*-style shirt, and my platforms. I didn't bring any sneakers on the trip because I didn't own any. I was the laughingstock. But it didn't bother me. This was me. My friends knew "that's Rachel, that's the way she is."

I still don't own a pair of sneakers. When I wear sneakers I become "cute." I don't want to be cute. I'd rather light myself on fire. Sneakers go against everything glamour. In my book, they should be limited to exercise.

That said, I realize sneakers, along with jeans, are an integral and inevitable staple of modern dressing. I also have to admit there are some pretty cool sneakers out there now. Not that I would ever be caught in any of them, but some of my friends and clients can work them pretty well. Mischa Barton looks adorable in her Keds. Puma and designers such as Stella McCartney have come out with styles that incorporate tweeds, metallics, and other unconventional fabrics for a more tailored but still sporty effect. The key is to go with a fashion-forward pair, keep them clean, and not make a habit of them.

On your day off, there are perfectly gorgeous choices in a flat or sandal. And some are made with all the comfort and support of a sneaker, making them a much chicer alternative.

day-off essentials

1. A great fitting pair of jeans (preferably in a dark wash).

2. A roomy jersey or cashmere constructed top (a better alternative to a T-shirt, yet just as comfy).

3. A wrap or shift dress in cotton, jersey, or another knit (that can be thrown on as quickly and comfortably as a T-shirt).

4. A tote, hobo, or some other roomy bag.

5. Nude or bare lip gloss (for a finish even without makeup).

6. Rosy cheek tint.

7. An all-season wrap or cardigan (that fits in your tote in case you get chilly).

8. A head scarf (in case hair needs to be pulled back or completely hidden).

9. Sunglasses.

10. Glam-on-the-go footwear (flats, boots, or wedges).

chapter 4
jet set

being a successful stylist means knowing how and what to pack for a trip and not forgetting the "style" in the rush to catch the plane.

When I relocated my home base from New York to Los Angeles in 2002, it was in part because so many of my pop star clients required my services on the West Coast, where much of the tour prepping, music videos, and photo shoots take place.

No sooner had I set up shop in L.A., and my client list shifted to Hollywood stars—and that meant getting back on an airplane to New York, Paris, and, gratefully, some exotic locales for editorial shoots, ad campaigns, runway shows, press junkets, and film premieres. I had to be ready for a quick trip at a moment's notice. For a magazine shoot with Salma Hayek, who was promoting her 2004 film with Pierce Bronson, *After the Sunset*, we flew to the Bahamas for all of twenty-four hours. For a film promotion, Lindsay Lohan and I went on a marathon tour through New York, London, Madrid, Paris, back to London, and then Berlin—all in ten days. I now spend nearly half my work schedule living out of hotels and collecting a substantial number of bonus miles.

Believe me, it's not as wonderful as it sounds. Not that I'm complaining. I mean, it's not a bad way to earn a living. I certainly learned straightaway how best to pack for the client and for myself when so much of our time is spent jet-setting the globe.

When packing my clients for a trip, I determine and fit much of what we need to glam them up for a press event way in advance. But even then, a backup look (or twenty) might be thrown in at the last minute—particularly extra heels and bags. The entire lot is carefully wrapped and stuffed with tissue paper and shipped by FedEx to its destination.

Well, almost the entire lot. When there's little room for a backup, my assistants or I might hand carry a gown on board. Take note: if you can't risk it because it's something valuable or you really love it, don't leave it to chance or baggage handlers who could accidentally send it off on a fourteen-hour flight to Pretoria. Take it with you as carry-on.

Of course, if it's a six-seater plane going to a photo shoot on a Caribbean island, the pilot himself might deny my bringing a gown, no matter how fabulous it is, into the tiny cabin. In those cases, you just have to hope for the best and pray that it arrives on the cargo flight.

Even far away from home, glamour doesn't take a holiday: Salma Hayek at the _After the Sunset_ premiere in New York in ombre silk Azzaro.

I also never ship the bling. Nor do I check it in. Ever. Unless the jewelry house itself delivers it, let's just say it's not unusual for me to be strip searched at the airport security check by officials questioning the bounty in one of my carry-on bags (always a Birkin and a black Gucci wheelie. My check-in luggage is by Diane von Furstenberg, because her luggage offers the perfect combination of durability and fashion). I can't really blame a security official for wondering why someone would need two dozen pairs of earrings, twenty bracelets, and ten whopper rings for a three-day trip.

My personal packing is a little less precious. Like yours, my life can run pretty madcap until the moment of liftoff, so I usually don't have the luxury of time. Instead I've learned to rely on the luxury of instinct, snap decision making, and experience to get me through it.

In my line of work, I've also learned all too well that a weekend trip can easily stretch into an eleven-day week. Once, a three-day trip to New York to style Jennifer Garner for her promos for *Alias* extended into eight days. Rebecca Romijn asked me to stay on for a fitting for her premiere of *X-Men: The Last Stand*, and then a few designers requested a couple of meetings with me to discuss concepts for upcoming projects. When I was finally packing to go home—Friday midday—a call came in from a higher power in the entertainment industry to get on his private jet that evening for Cannes. Let's just say that when this individual makes a request, you accept it immediately and with grace.

Thankfully I had my cropped black mink shrug and three cases of my favorite personal jewelry. Yes, I'd packed that much when I thought it would only be a three-day trip. Although jewelry houses give me access to some great options for my clients,

My baby kickin' it in Cannes

DVF before lunch on her yacht.

A universe away from the boardroom:
Russell Simmons and Tamara Mellon

Postcard from Cannes

My dear Brian Atwood and I met a decade ago
in Paris when we both leaped up on a table and
began dancing! He's as dreamy looking as ever.

A very relaxed Harvey Weinstein
and his sweet Georgina Chapman

Fashion has to meet function when I'm working, so (yet another) Missoni caftan allows for plenty of movement and comfort . . .

sometimes nothing works better than a vintage piece or two from my personal collection. And fortunately three of my favorite vintage stores were within a three-block radius of my hotel. I ran over in the pouring rain and snatched fifteen dresses for myself.

Even if you board a jet only once a year, take it from a frequent flier:

- *Determine and fit clothes well in advance.*

- *If you can ship anything ahead by FedEx, UPS, or DHL, do it.*

- *If you can't risk it getting lost, carry it on board.*

- *Be flexible. If you forgot something, go shopping. Never forgo an opportunity because you have nothing to wear.*

. . .so, too, does this cozy shrug over a Michael Kors dress on Debra Messing.

no time to let it go

As you no doubt have it ingrained in your mind by this chapter, there is glamour even in comfort. We've all heard the endless nostalgia for the golden years of travel, when airlines employed the genius of Pucci, Halston, and Valentino to elegantly suit up the crew, and travelers didn't look like they had just rolled out of bed. But hope prevails in modern travel, as cabins are filling up with attendants clad in uniforms by Christian Lacroix, Richard Tyler, and Julien Macdonald, and a small yet growing force of frequent fliers are embracing casual luxe on the road. Jet-setting, even if you're sitting in economy class, is an ideal opportunity to flex this approach.

Going on holiday doesn't mean taking a vacation from stylishly living it up. You never know who you might run into at the airport or on plane. It could be someone you're dying to work with. Or it could be The One and you could fall madly in love. My sister met her love on a plane from Miami to Los Angeles. It can happen!

I'm not suggesting that you wear high heel boots and a full face of makeup. You'll only end up arriving with puffy ankles, unable to walk, and smudged eyes and dried skin, unable to face the world. But on holiday my style radar doesn't shut off. In fact, I find my best inspiration when I'm away from official business and really able to indulge in my surroundings. I love watching the way locals and visitors put together their clothes and accessories, and how they strike a pose, in them. I even get to shop for myself finally.

It's true that styling celebrities has turned into a year-round affair, as the awards season has spread out to three-fourths of the calendar year and demand has heightened for PYFTs (pretty, young, and famous things) to appear at the openings of designers' flagship retail temples or to sit front-row at a runway show. Any excuse for a fashion moment.

But I still manage a quickie holiday between the announcement of the nominees for the Golden Globes

At the Venice Film Fest with Lindsay and the Missoni clan: Francesco and Margherita with their uncle Vittorio in the middle.

in mid-December and the start of the couture shows the following month. It's usually St. Barths. I adore the fantasy aspect of the place. It's so unreal: the yachts in the marina, the gold-draped Bain de Soleil beauties, the very chicness of it all even when everyone is so underdressed. I absolutely lap it up. I can be with twenty friends at a delicious seafood bistro in the evening and the next morning get away to a private beach with Rodger. We've been going to St. Barths nearly every year since our honeymoon in 1998.

But that seven- or ten-day holiday happens for me only once a year. During the summer months, I try to get in an extended weekend. It saves my sanity, and I highly recommend it. I try to squeeze in an escape to the south of France during July 4 before hitting Paris for the couture shows. Or there's gorgeous Sardinia around Labor Day. From there, it's right into New York for fashion week (where I'm running off either to see or style a show).

Everyone needs time off. It's important to have a special spot you can escape to for a weekend or a week. Exploring new cities is great, but there's also something comforting in going to a fabulous home away from home. Don't have one yet? Consider where you've always dreamed of spending a few inspiring afternoons and evenings and book it. Even if it's a year away before you fly there, your daily outlook will change from just counting down the days to liftoff.

flight gear

The crew has their uniform, and stylish travelers have theirs, too.

Be it holiday or work, my flight gear is the same. I'm always in black. I wear cotton jersey wide-leg pants or leggings and a comfy cotton jersey top. To keep cozy, I choose from a fur vest, a great cashmere wrap, or a chunky, oversized sweater. Then I have a silk scarf to wrap around my head if the hair goes all wrong or around my neck if there's a chill.

The key is in the layering. It always seems to be so stuffy in the airport and too cold on the plane. And despite the weather report, it could all flip by the time the jet touches down nine hours later.

A pair of big sunglasses comes in very handy during the actual getting between points A and B. I use them as an eye mask when I sleep—and even when I'm not actually dozing but want to keep a chatty fellow traveler from interrupting my peace. Think of them as a do-not-disturb sign to keep the skies friendly. Big dark shades can hide tired, bloodshot eyes in the fluorescent-lit airport terminals, too. All the flying I've done for work these last few years has made me intimately familiar with just how red "red-eye" can be.

With my niece Sophie in the Hamptons

My sister, Pamela, with her son, Sophie's big brother, Luke

Despite all the jewelry in my cases, I wear very little on board—maybe the wishbone on a chain that Rodger gave me, a pair of light hoops in gold, my engagement and wedding rings, and always, always my watch. Too much jewelry calls attention to yourself, which in some airports and cities can be hazardous to your safety. It can also be annoying to you or fellow passengers, with big earrings getting tangled as you sleep or bangles clanging away. Even in first class, an airplane is too compact a space not to exercise manners.

On land or in the air, my bag is big. For traveling, it's essential for holding a scarf, sunglasses, and the following:

- *An oversized pocketbook for passport and tickets, as well as receipts, business cards, and so on.*

- *A hard calendar, instead of a techie device. With schedules changing so much, writing it down as it happens can be helpful. Some things are better left to pen and paper.*

- *A digital camera (which I can spot immediately in the black hole interior of my bag because of its hot pink and red vintage Pucci case).*

- *Moisturizer and eye cream.*

- *A toothbrush and toothpaste.*

- *Mints/gum.*

- *Magazines and other reading materials.*

- *A favorite scent to be applied after the flight. Carry a travel-sized oil or fragrance and resist spritzing anything before you walk off the plane.*

- *Antibacterial wipes and tissues.*

- *Neosporin for dabbing at the nostrils' edge to keep them from getting dry and to block germs.*

- *A small mirror and a bag of cosmetic basics (cheek tint, lip gloss, mascara, and concealer) to apply just before landing.*

leader of the pack

When it comes to luggage, aim for streamline. Go with cases you can haul effortlessly by yourself. Resist overpacking. Don't be the amateur who holds up a plane because your luggage is too heavy or is too large to fit in the overhead compartment.

All your luggage should coordinate. Money shouldn't be an issue here, either, because there are many charming and inexpensive cases out there. You can find great luggage on any budget. Or you can always go all black. Neither you nor your luggage should look like a mishmash.

Think of an eye mask as a do-not-disturb sign to keep the skies friendly.

When I'm traveling for a week or more, I tend to take two suitcases—a big one for my clothes and a slightly smaller one for shoes and bags. But whenever possible, I aim for one case. Remember, the phrase is "on the go."

Always keep jewelry and other valuables on board with you. Keep your cosmetic kit in your carry-on, too, or have a separate hard case that checks in with the rest of the luggage. A cracked lotion bottle or crushed eye shadow case can really crimp a trip. To that end, always contain leakable products in resealable plastic bags—even in your make-up case. Pack a few extra bags for the return trip home.

PACKING ORDER

The contents of your main cases should offer a semblance of order to what is probably a time of madness in your life, whether the ticket is to paradise or payday.

- *Start with shoes on the bottom. I put mine in sacks, either those that come with the shoes or other drawstring cloth bags, so they don't get scratched. Protect their shape by stuffing them with socks, tank tops, or something else you are taking with you.*

- *The next layer is any jeans, folded in half.*

chairman of the *on board*

*Few designers epitomize the jet-set lifestyle more in their fashion collections or personal life than one of my all-American favorites, **Michael Kors**, who knows what to carry on board with singular panache.*

I don't think anyone's rushing back to the days of traveling in a skirt suit and pumps. Comfort is too important to us now. But there should still be a sense of looking good when you arrive. This is a very public moment, even if you're not a public figure.

Modern travel is not necessarily packing steamer trunks of clothes. It's about having the right accoutrements. Even if you're in coach or on a two-hour flight, you can turn a trip into your own little spa experience. With a few indulgences, the whole travel process will feel better.

For starters, never get on a plane without a cashmere blanket or oversized cashmere scarf. Store it in your tote and then pull it out when the cabin becomes chilly. Nothing looks better tied around your shoulders. And if a Birkin is not in your budget, even a huge monogrammed L.L. Bean tote is great.

Rather than dealing with a coat, which is always a bulky mess even if it fits in the overhead compartment, opt for a great, heavy sweater with a tank top underneath. I always carry a black cashmere crew neck on the plane. You can sleep in it. And if the temperature is warm upon arrival, you can tie the sweater around your waist.

If you're not into tank tops, then go with a black T-shirt. It's all I wear when I travel. Black T-shirts can go under a suit or over a bathing suit. They travel well in any climate.

Always have a fabulous eye mask. Everyone can afford that. Maybe you can't afford a sable coat, but you can afford a silk eye mask. I mean, who wants to wear those stiff nylon ones supplied by the airlines?

Don't get on a plane with a lot of makeup. Keep it to lip gloss and moisturizer and you'll look all the better when you arrive. Wear a neat pair of flip-flops or Birkenstock mules. They're the easiest to slip in and out of through security. Keep a pair of cashmere socks in the tote in case your toes get cold on the plane.

Don't forget to pack a pair of sunglasses. You never want to walk through an airport without them. They're a girl's best friend, particularly after a red-eye flight. I'm also a big believer in hats. It can even be a crunchable, funny canvas bucket hat in your tote.

Pack DVDs and an iPod and whatever reading you need to catch up on. Like me, I'm sure you don't want to deal with someone else's selections on the plane.

You might never end up on a tabloid cover, but a little bit of luxury can look good and make your travels more comfortable. And that's very modern.

mischa barton *on a bon voyage*

I love to travel, and I do quite a lot of it throughout the year, particularly to Paris, New York, and London. I was born in London and have family there, so I visit at least twice a year. I go for holidays to Hawaii, Ireland, Mexico, and Morocco. But I don't just travel there because they're pretty places. I go more for the cultural experience. I also spent a month living in Toronto for the filming of *Closing the Ring*. So, I guess you could say I'm pretty mobile.

Forever on the go, Mischa and her dark sunnies

I'm a big believer in using travel agents. They take care of all the details, which is a relief whether the trip is for work or pleasure.

For short trips, like L.A. to New York, I try to make it only carry-on. If the trip is going to last more than three days, I may have to do check-in luggage. If it's a month or more away from L.A., where I live, then I may have to bring three suitcases. It's a consequence of the job that I need all those shoes and bags and clothing options for parties and dinners.

On holiday, I definitely try to keep it to one case and light. I never take more than I can carry. I'll pack a few extra changes if I'm going to be on the beach every day, and definitely some nighttime options. I always leave extra room because I know I'll bring lots of new things home with me.

I like very generic black cases—even my Louis Vuitton cases have black covers—because I want my luggage to look like everyone else's. If I have two or more cases, I'll usually pack shoes in one of them. If all I'm checking in is one case, I'll pack the shoes at the bottom, then layer according to weight, with the lighter, delicate things on top. I'll stuff any electrical cords and books on the sides or in pockets. Any dressier dresses or nicer things will go in either carry-on cases or hanger bags.

I hate getting stopped or delayed at the security gate, so I make sure tweezers, scissors, and anything else that can hold me up at the checkpoint is stored away in the checked-in luggage. My tickets, passport, and iPod all go in accessible pockets in my purse. Once on board, I keep my purse and laptop where I can easily reach them.

- *Then layer everything else, laying it flat with as few folds as possible: trousers, sweaters, dresses. On top, place the more fragile items—anything chiffon, beaded, sequined— turned inside out so they won't catch. I also wrap these pieces in plastic (the bags you get from the dry-cleaners work great) or tissue paper.*

- *Lastly, no matter how tempting, don't overstuff your bags. Clothes and even shoes end up badly creased. The extra weight can cost you extra dollars at check-in, not to mention incur brutal treatment from baggage handlers, and the case is more likely to explode on the conveyer belt. It just looks bad.*

Always unpack your bags as soon as you arrive at your lodgings. This gives clothes and shoes a chance to air out and regain shape. It also enables you to see everything you have right away, hanging in the closet or tucked away in the drawers—including what may be missing before a meeting or event.

in the bag

What you pack, of course, depends on where you're going, for how long, and, most important, the weather report!

Who your traveling companions are, too, can determine what's inside a suitcase:

- *Single girlfriends: sexy dresses, high heels, and lots of jewelry for a riot of a time.*

- *Family: more comfortable outfits, and not as many options, because you can repeat looks with your family.*

- *Significant others: their favorite things and yours, including those little nothings that could make your trip sexier.*

- *Business associates: business attire that doesn't easily wrinkle, including a dressy option in case dinner follows the big meetings.*

city dressing

Life is about diversity. So when I'm spending any amount of time in a city, I tend to make like the locals while I'm there. If you're feeling a different way in a different environment, go with it.

In Paris, I like to dress more graphic, in crisp, white shirts with black trousers and a cinched waist belt.

In New York, I tend to dress up more than in L.A. (where white replaces black and I live in jersey pants and off-the-shoulder Missoni tunics). I go full on with, say, a Chanel jacket with trousers, or a Lanvin dress and boots. I do more fashion by day and darker colors—red, chocolate, black—by night.

In London, as in New York, I take along a few beautiful long coats. I also push the fashion envelope because the London vibe is more structured, edgy, and androgynous. I'll rock trousers with a fitted jacket and vest, like a sexy three-piece suit.

In St. Barths or St. Tropez, it's caftans daily over bikinis, with wedges or espadrilles, and gold jewelry everywhere. And my sunnies, of course.

The Hamptons, where my family gathers, is very pared down, very relaxed. Metallic pumps would just be stupid. Instead I slip into wedges (high, of course) along with pretty sundresses, and oversized sweaters at night. Nothing structured, just very flowing, almost romantic choices.

MAKINGS OF A BON VOYAGE

Purpose: Business

Weather Report: Hot or cold

Pack: Separates that can be mixed and matched as complete professional outfits—a white blouse that can go with a skirt suit and jeans; a pretty camisole to go underneath the blouse or alone with a jacket; a three-piece suit in which the vest can be worn after hours alone, without a blouse. The goal is not to be weighed down since you might have to rush off a plane and straight into a meeting. Go with wrinkle-resistant fabrics: natural fibers like silk and wool keep well, as do natural/synthetic blends such as wool/viscose. Knitwear crinkles less than woven fabrics. Avoid checking in luggage if possible, and opt for a hanging bag. Don't forget to keep the briefcase really chic and coordinating.

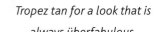

Purpose: Holiday

Weather Report: Hot

Pack: Bikinis, cute bras, and boy shorts to wear under sheer dresses (and that can double as swimwear when the moment arises); tunics, caftans, and sundresses that can serve as dresses or tops. A fabulous belt can turn a sarong into a dress, so pack one that sits on the waist, in leather or raffia, or a colored woven or gold chain. Anything in lighter, brighter colors, and definitely white, is appropriate, and leave most of the black and any items that require dry-cleaning at home. Leave the pumps behind, too. This is one of the few times I'll pack flip-flops, and a sandal of any kind is requisite. Also great are espadrilles and open-toe wedges. Clothes might be minimal, but not accessories. Stockpile hoops, anything ethnic, and bangles (island cheapies are such a great addition). And layer yellow gold on top of a St. Tropez tan for a look that is always überfabulous.

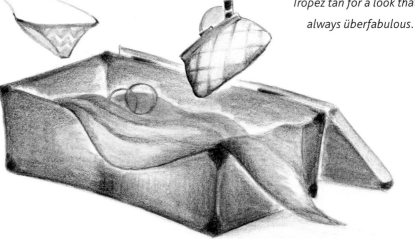

Purpose: Holiday

Weather Report: Cold

Pack: Stick to the basics or your suitcase will bulk up quickly. That includes color. Black, brown, and cream are best. Start with a great turtleneck, preferably cashmere, because it's the warmest and least bulky, and a sexier plunging V-neck sweater. Think layers, such as tank tops and silky camisoles. You'll need jeans, of course, as well as black trousers and a skirt in a cut—pencil or full—that's right for your shape. A light dress is okay, depending on the coat; otherwise go with a wool or other heavier fabric in a sexy silhouette. Pack hosiery, but never skin-colored. Don't forget a belt or two to cinch in bulky sweaters or dresses at the hips or waist, and a wrap that can double as a scarf or shawl. A bolero or fur shrug or vest (faux or real) glams up any outfit. If there's room, pack two coats, one dressy and one more casual (personally, I always go with a white or cream coat over a black one because it looks richer, more exciting in that Dr. Zhivago sort of way). Don't forget a hat (a newsboy, a beanie cap, a floppy wool beret— anything that folds away), gloves, and even sunglasses (to stave off the blinding sunlight bouncing off the snow).

This is no time to overlook shoes either. Go with a comfortable yet chic pair of walking shoes that can survive through rain and snow, be it a wedge boot, a patent rubber flat boot, or even a fur-lined après-ski boot.

on the slopes

I know it's hard to feel sexy in skiwear when you imagine yourself resembling the Stay Puft Marshmallow Man. And you cannot wear a heel at a ski resort. You just can't. I'm the queen of heels, but there are some places where they are off limits.

I've been skiing since I was four, so I know a thing or two about the sport and the culture. The sense of freedom on the top of the mountain is unlike anything else. I may no longer be the downhill daredevil I once was, but I am still conscious about form—on and off the slopes.

For me the uniform is bold and graphic. I love a silk-satin nylon black or white jacket with a fur-trimmed hood and tight, black stretch pants. Karl Lagerfeld's snowbound creations for Chanel are perfection. With skis off, a wedge or moon boot cuts a sharp look. Sport can be a little glam, too.

FINAL CALL

A trip can be just a trip. Or it can be an experience with happy returns. Whether it is work or a holiday, make the most of it. Grab a few winks on the flight between meetings in two cities. There's luxury in a silk mask, as Michael Kors points out, as well as the personal time on board away from cell phones or PDAs. Have a glass of champagne and catch up on trashy tabloids and fashion magazines. At your destination, after the workday is done, treat yourself to a meal at the hottest new restaurant or a massage at the hotel spa.

Traveling stylishly is the height of glamour—words to live by while hovering a mile high in the sky.

chapter 5

lip gloss and mane toss

I'm a firm believer in the adage that it is what's on the inside that ultimately counts. I mean, who doesn't subscribe to that? But there is plenty of virtue in aesthetics, too. And a smear of lip gloss and a bang-up haircut can have powerful results both inside *and* out.

Beauty should be a part of your everyday glamour routine. Cosmetics, hair, and skin care merit as much regard as a well-tailored dress or a perfect pair of sunglasses. This is why I always keep an emergency makeup bag and a head scarf in my purse. It's why I encourage my clients, and remind myself, to squeeze in that mani-pedi no matter how crazed the schedule. And it's why, no matter how many girls I dress for the red carpet on a given awards day, or how exhausted I may be, I never hit the pillow without first cleansing my face.

None of this has to be complicated. A hairstyle should never resemble a wedding cake. Makeup shouldn't come off as clownish drag. Too much of a good thing can only age you. So keep the hand light and the choices few when it comes to cosmetics and hair products to avoid looking spent and scary. At the very least, your product load should appear minimal to the untrained observer, because even a "natural" look requires concealer, foundation, eye shadow, mascara, blusher, brow gel, and lip gloss in nude and rose shades. Hardly au natural.

My mom has always been very big on makeup, but she advised I dabble in moderation. Not that I always listened. I went to high school during the super-sized 1980s, and I was very into heaps of zinc pink gloss, wide swaths of frosty blue

eye shadow, and layers of colored mascara—
way too much of everything! I thought more
was better, that it made me look older.

Now that I am older, I try not to wear
too much. I've learned some valuable tips from
the makeup artists I work with, like how too
much frost enhances wrinkles; to always even
skin tone with the right shade of foundation;
and to beware of under-eye concealer that is
too white. I get raccoon eyes very easily when
I don't get enough sleep (which is often during
the awards season), but going too light can be
just as frightening looking.

My idea of "natural beauty" is one best
appreciated via the prism of 1970s style: a
smoky eye, a mess of long, highlighted hair, an
all-over deep tan, and lips glossy with a hint
of gold. But my rule is this: if you don't look
kissable, then scrub it off and start over.

With Marc Jacobs after his fall 2008 show: Keep
makeup to a minimum for smooch appeal.

Rebecca Romijn just before a shoot in Los Angeles, 2005

And if your 'do is a certified don't, then start over there, too. Case in point: I came back from camp one summer such a changed twelve-year-old that my parents didn't even recognize me. I had doused my hair with a whole bottle of Sun-In and it turned a nice, brassy orange. The foibles of youth! My mom drove me straight to Vidal Sassoon, where I got a bob—the last time my hair was above my shoulders—and the first of many, many color treatments.

My long hair is signature to my look, but it's not set permanently. I lighten and highlight and darken according to my mood. Some of my clients are a bit more extreme, like Lindsay Lohan, who changes her hair color as enthusiastically as her gowns on Oscar night. She adores fashion, and part of her love affair is flirting with hair color and makeup. Whether a change is slight or significant, what matters is that it happens at all. Beauty is one area where consulting with experienced professionals can make all the difference. Even fifteen minutes in the chair at the department store beauty counter can change your life.

It takes a village to create a star. I've collaborated with a community of pros gifted enough to transform an actress who's burning it at both ends into a photo-worthy main attraction. Among them are this chapter's VIPs: makeup artist Paul Starr, hairstylist Andy LeCompte, and my personal go-to hair and makeup virtuoso, Byron Williams.

A vision of perfection: Mischa's secret is her typically light hand with makeup and hair and nails kept short and polished.

Beauty chameleon Lindsay Lohan as a blonde with waves...

...and seeing straight red.

face time

Paul Starr embodies his name. He not only resembles a rock star, he has also painted some of the most iconic faces in the style business, from Madonna to David Bowie, and he's worked with countless major fashion houses, magazines, and the most legendary photographers and video directors. He has his own book, too, and a cosmetics line in development. Together, we've glammed up Lindsay Lohan, Salma Hayek, and Jennifer Garner. Here, Paul reveals his insights on giving good face, day or evening:

I've been in the industry long enough to know that makeup has to be appropriate for the person as well as the moment. So always consider the context. Are you heading to the office? Or the red carpet? No two faces should be made up alike.

When I see women go out without makeup, I think, "What is the point?" Sometimes I see a woman applying foundation in her car, or eyeliner while looking into a tiny compact mirror. If this is you, stop. Make the time for a beauty ritual, even if it's just five minutes. Use proper light, get a routine down, and learn what's right for you. Go to the makeup counter, to a friend, get a book (this one is a good start), or if need be, hire someone.

When it comes to cosmetics, be willing to experiment. Play. Have fun. Women tend to get stuck in ruts, becoming too comfortable with whatever worked for them in college.

But don't be afraid to change with the times! If it doesn't look good, what's the worst that can happen? You just wash it off. Makeup is not rocket science. But it does take a little testing and practice.

The rules of attraction include putting your best face forward, whether it's to get a job or a new mate. You owe it to yourself. It's the only face you have, so make the best of it.

- *On skin: I'm a firm believer in keeping good skin. Skin is your best asset. You should develop a good skin regimen that works for you. Save on the foundation and spend the extra coins on skin care.*

- *On foundation: It's there to even everything out—not mask it. That's why I'm a fan of tinted moisturizers with SPF. It's all right there in a single bottle. Match your neck and chest. Hands are usually a little darker since they get much more*

Makeup artist Paul Starr

don't leave home without it: paul starr's ingredients for the cosmetics bag-to-go

- Concealer
- Sunblock moisturizer/tinted moisturizer with SPF 15
- Eyelash curler
- Two pencils: a dark brown for the eye and another that matches your natural lip tone
- Lip color: stick or stain, one that matches your natural lip tone
- Crème blusher
- Shimmer stick
- Mascara
- A good lip balm with a bit of gloss

exposure to the sun, so they tend not to be great guides. When you are shopping for foundation, wear a low-cut blouse. But once you score your perfect match, never slather it on your neck. Foundation doesn't belong on your clothes. Blend and blend at the jaw line to avoid a border.

- *On concealers: Have two. One should match your skin tone; the other should be a shade lighter, but not too much lighter. I keep a palette ready in case of tanning or other skin tone changes.*

- *On colors: Never match makeup to clothing. So boring. Too many women think that if they wear an orange dress they should go with peach eye shadow and orangey lips. You never want to match. You're wearing the outfit—it's not wearing you (or at least it better not). Choose colors that complement your skin tone, eye, and hair color.*

- *On shimmers: All should not glitter gold, bronze, or whatever metallic you're sparkling the night in. Go with either a shimmering eye or a shimmering lip—but not both. The alternate feature can go matte.*

- *On blending: This is an underrated step that can make all the difference. A lip pencil should create shape, not a border, so draw the outline and then blend until the focus is on the pucker. The same goes with blushers. Mimic a postcoital flush by applying blush at the center of the cheeks, then feathering it out and upward until a diffused hint of color remains at the perimeter.*

- *On gloss: Translucent or opaque, frost or stain, lip gloss can be the sexy finisher to any look. It can also moisturize and plump. But too much of the stuff, and it begins dripping to sloppy, porn-star effect. There's nothing sexy about that.*

- *On eyes: An alluring eye, even for day, usually views the world from a palette of golds, taupes, browns, rusts. But resist highlighting above the crease. An obvious frost there looks old-fashioned.*

For evening, emphasize a smoldering eye with pale, kissable lips.

- *On brows: Always keep them groomed. Go to a professional—even if it's only once. A professional will teach you what to do. Tweeze them regularly. Brush them daily (a clean toothbrush works well).*

DAY FACE

Start with a light moisturizer (tinted or not), but one with a minimum of 15 SPF. Even if you prefer a foundation, go with the lightest formula possible, especially for day. A cake face is not pretty.

Brush brows. Then outline the top eyelid with a pencil and feather the color with a light fingertip smudge or brush. If you have light hair or fair skin tone, go with a dark brown pencil; dark hair and olive skin can take black. Apply a little eye shadow. Stroke a paler shade on the lid, a darker shade along the crease. Curl lashes. Apply black mascara to the top lashes and brown mascara along the bottom.

To cheeks, apply a shade close to your skin's natural flush. I prefer crème for day. It's more modern. Powders can look cakey, but if you have oily skin, it's the better option. Reapply throughout the day as needed.

Finish off your day face at the lips. Go natural with a bit of gloss. Or if you prefer color, start with a pencil and create a natural lip shape and feather inward. Stain the lip with a color that is the same shade or slightly darker than the pencil (remember: no outline should be visible). Blot. Dab a bit of gloss in the center and press lips together lightly.

EVENING (OR RED CARPET) FACE

Always begin with a clean face. You can skip the SPF after the sun goes down, but don't skimp on the moisturizer, be it tinted or under a light foundation. The next steps depend on whether the emphasis is on the eyes or lips.

THE EYES HAVE IT

Nighttime begs for a bit more, so line the top of the lid and underneath the bottom lashes of the eye with a smoky pencil. Go stronger than with the daytime eyeliner, but not so bold that it looks like a 1950s eye. Feather with a fingertip or brush.

From the eye shadow palette, use the darker shade used during the day along the crease and apply it to the entire lid. Keep much more of a focus on the outside corners of the eye.

Curl lashes. Use volume-building mascara with a thickening formula for the top and bottom lashes for a more defined look. Cheeks also intensify a degree in the evening with a slightly deeper shade. A glam accent is a shimmer stick in white or gold. Dab with a finger or brush right on the cheekbone, right above the apple, close to where the eyebrow ends. With such a strong eye, keep the lip nearly nude with a gloss.

LIP SERVICE

If the focus is on the lips, pencil them in a shade that is the same or slightly lighter than the lipstick or gloss. Feather the outline and stain in any shade of wine, from sangria red to a deep burgundy.

Flush cheeks with a lighter shade.

Keep eyes fairly minimal and clean: a shimmer stick along the lid and several coats of mascara. Experiment with a strong violet mascara for drama.

lipstick traces: red or dead

Anne Hathaway's signature ruby lips

Few sleights of hand work as magically (or is it miraculously?) as red lipstick.

My first play at the stuff was in my mother's bathroom. I wanted big lips, so I took her red lipstick and proceeded to run it all over my face. I was five. I went through all kinds of frosts and glosses during my teens, but I also harnessed the power of red when I really wanted to make a statement. By the time I moved to New York in my early twenties, my look was totally pale skin and really red lipstick. Even now, tan as I am, red remains a key element in my color box.

Red lipstick *is* glamour. A little mascara and red lips and you're good to go. Every woman should have a red in her bag at all times. There's a shade for everybody. If you're tan or olive, glide on an earthy red with orange or brown undertones. If your skin is pale, choose one with bluer tones.

No matter how dead you look or feel, red lipstick can instantly liven up your look and mood. It's a crowd pleaser. It's sexy. It never goes out of style.

scents of style

Nothing in your beauty arsenal should overpower you, and that includes your scent. Notes that attract flattery to a friend might fall flat on you, so choose personally and choose wisely.

- *At the fragrance counter, start by spritzing your wrist. A scent isn't going to smell the same in thin air or on a tester card as it does once it hits your skin. Body temperature affects a fragrance's notes, and each of us has our own specific skin chemistry. So what smells sexy on a friend may smell sickly on you. Try before you buy.*

- *Don't rub your wrists together. This crushes the scent.*

- *Walk away. Some notes are immediately strong while others are revealed hours later. Give the spritz and yourself time before you make a purchase. If there are complimentary samples, even better.*

- *Don't buy a scent based on a celebrity endorsement. Choose it because it truly suits you.*

- *Once you find your magic potion, stock up on it. Create a fragrance wardrobe, with one for day, another for evening. Spray on a lighter juice for summer, something more baroque for winter. I prefer the clean, earthier scents of amber, tuberose, and gardenia. My aversion to clothes that are too sweet extends to fragrances. You don't want to give yourself, or everyone around you, a headache by marinating in it. But don't reserve fragrance for your neck or wrist either. Scent rises, so dab some on your ankles or behind the knees.*

You want to smell like a woman—sexy and alluring. There are classic choices, of course: it's said that Ava Gardner had her Acqua di Parma, the author Colette and the bombshell Brigitte Bardot loved Jicky by Guerlain, and Josephine Baker smelled of Joy by Jean Patou. And we've all rhapsodized over the iconic image of Marilyn Monroe splashing on Chanel No. 5—all of these fragrances are rich in notes and history.

reality check: jennifer garner

Everyday beauty? I confess, I normally don't do a lot. I don't wear makeup every day. And what I do wear depends on how much of a hurry I'm in.

Mostly it's just enough to look presentable and for me to feel good. I dab some concealer under the eyes and around the nose where I get a little red. For color, I apply a little blush on the cheeks and on the eye bone. Then mascara. And I'm good to go.

It's not always so bare bones, of course. Makeup, in particular, is so key. It absolutely changes everything. The single thing Paul Starr does is not use too much foundation—just enough to make skin look glowing. He never cakes it on, but sponges it where it's needed. He finds one area to focus on—either a great sweep of eyeliner or a bright lip. But never both. Just as Rachel has encouraged me to play with new looks when it comes to red carpet gowns, Paul has taught me to be more playful with makeup. Nothing's permanent, so have fun with it.

One of my favorite moments when the beauty and dress all came together was the 2004 Academy Awards. Rachel got me into this beautiful, one-shoulder coral dress by Valentino. It was very simple, very clean, almost athletic. I never like things to be over the top. I feel silly. Paul also kept the makeup restrained, but pretty. And Oscar Blandi just brushed my hair back into a bun, leaving loose bangs. I felt glamorous, but still me.

When it comes to my skin care, it depends on my mood. Sometimes, I go through weeks when I love the toner and everything in a given prescribed routine. Then I go for the basics. What I don't ever do without is cream under the eyes and a moisturizer with SPF. I always do my face, and I never, ever skip my neck. *Muy importante.*

American beauty: Jennifer Garner on a photo shoot in Malibu, 2005

making the part with andy lecompte

As much as Mischa, Nicole, and Lindsay are chameleons in clothes, these girls also love to tease out new personas through their coifs. Our friend and hairstylist Andy LeCompte recognizes this implicitly. Once, he convinced Nicole to slash her long hair into a bob. He let Mischa have her way with longer locks she can bundle up or brush out. And he helped Lindsay rally her inner Brigitte Bardot one night, then Ann-Margret the next. Here Andy dishes on dos and don'ts:

Why care about good hair? Because when hair is "done"—whether that means a new cut and color or something more involved—the change isn't just in the mirror. You feel better. You feel more polished, more together, and you feel more powerful. One of my clients is a film director, and she always gets her hair cut and colored right before starting a new job.

A completely new cut stokes another perspective for you and others. The bob I gave Nicole could be worn straight or wavy. It also gave her a more sophisticated look, influencing the way the public perceived her. Nicole is always game to take a risk, but this shorter hairstyle announced to the world the new phase she was entering.

There are plenty of risks, though, that are just plain traumatic. Overdose on too much product like hair spray or gel and hair is stiff and not sexy. The lighter your hand, the

fresher and better your hair will look. Go with hair that moves.

Overhighlighting is also harmful to your look, not to mention the health of your hair. Blonderexia isn't just a California girl's disorder. It's probably happened to someone you know. Get them to a good colorist and fast.

Like cuts and style, color is also something that should never remain the same. Extremes work on few people of any age and can become trickier with each decade. Harsh color is not flattering. Faces framed by super platinum blonde or raven brunette hair usually require more makeup, which can present an even harder appearance. Most women (and men) can't go wrong with warmer hair tones.

Then there's just overdoing it. Remember: the louder the outfit, the quieter the hair and makeup should be. The simpler the outfit, the more you can play up hair and makeup.

Andy LeCompte and me off the clock at a pre-Oscar party, 2007

hair extensions

At home base in L.A. or on tour with the likes of Madonna, Andy LeCompte shares the key tools to work your locks.

- A Mason Pearson hairbrush—this rubber cushion-padded tool is essential for blow-drying, brushing out straight or wavy hair, backcombing, and teasing.

- Wide-tooth plastic comb—to keep wet hair from breaking.

- Round brush with boar bristles—for blow-drying hair.

- Curling iron with either ¾ or 1-inch rod.

- Ceramic flat iron—straighten hair, or make messy waves by wrapping hair around the iron and twisting.

- Lightweight hair serum—for shine and taming.

- Clay wax—a pomade without shine that gives hair texture. Good to separate and define ends.

- Hair spray—if you're a regular user, go with a better quality spray or risk damaging hair. Worth every cent is L'Oreal's Elnett.

- Shampoo and conditioner—choose a quality duo, but no need to rinse and repeat!

- Dry shampoo—for emergencies, but it also adds volume and texture to otherwise clean hair.

- Detox shampoo—use once every two weeks to remove build-up.

SPLITTING HAIRS

There used to be a rule that as you add on the years, you should lop off the hair length. But I don't think that applies anymore. There are so many other factors to consider when it comes to hair, and age hardly registers on my list. Look at Grace Coddington. Somewhere south of sixty, she's as beautiful as ever with that wavy, cinnamon fleece that falls below her shoulders.

No matter the length, a sleepy bang that sweeps over the eye is always a sexy, mysterious touch. Any sort of fringe, from the short to the cheekbone, can register such a reaction if you play it right.

Pulled-back hair is always chic for the office or a party, and only requires a few pins. A polished, low ponytail can also be the way to go in a professional setting, while the undone style of a loose chignon is a great pairing with formal wear. Even hair that's long and loose like Rachel's requires some effort. But it doesn't need much investment in time and attention every morning if it's well cut.

Each face demands a style of its own. There are physical features to consider, along with personality, attitude, and lifestyle. Work with a stylist you completely trust to figure out a cut that softens and frames your face. Don't force a style, but be willing to experiment. You've only got one face. Never cover it up.

skin deep

I love a tan. I love a deep, Bain de Soleil–like tan, rich with all the promise of St. Tropez and Ipanema and Marrakesh. I tend to keep bronzed through the year, a consequence of my having olive skin that soaks up the sun year-round in Los Angeles. I don't fake bake. I soak the rays directly from the source. And I don't make any apologies for it.

Obviously, I'm not going to recommend you walk in my heels on this one. There has been plenty of progress in over-the-counter products and spray tans that can color you in shades other than tangy orange. After tight updos, another instant killer to an otherwise drop-dead look is an obvious fake bake. Several weeks of work on a couture gown were ruined one time when a makeup artist who will remain unnamed convinced a certain young star to undergo the spray. It was too much, too fast. She was the color of burnt sienna. The extra-long platinum extensions the hair stylist gave her only added insult to injury. It was a case of beauty overkill.

A blatantly artificial tan is never good for the red carpet, let alone life. If it doesn't look real, then you're better off pasty white.

Tan or not, an SPF-enriched moisturizer is nonnegotiable. So is a daily skin cleansing and care regimen, whatever it might be for your particular skin, schedule, and budget. Regular facials are incredibly consequential, too. Five minutes every night on your own and an hour whenever possible under your aesthetician's skilled fingers are more than just good skin care. They can provide meditative moments from outside realities, a chance to silently reflect and just be with yourself. And that's just as beauty beneficial as a good crème.

byron williams

With two salons in Los Angeles and a budding signature hair care and styling line, Byron Williams still manages to keep it festive when he races over on any given morning or evening to spruce me up for a photo shoot or big bash. The guy's a double whammy, too, able to wield both a hairbrush and a makeup brush in a single sitting. As he puts it, "Isn't that what most of you glamazons do every day?"

BYRON'S BEAUTY BASICS

1 Evian water spray to spritz hair and skin.

2 La Prairie eye cream to perk up tired eyes.

3 Dry shampoo spray—Klorane—for clean-looking hair in a snap or to give a thicker texture.

4 YSL bronzer for a healthy glow.

5 Epicurean pro-collagen lotion—a little bit here or there when you're tired and readying to go out. Pumps you up.

6 Byron hair spray—Rachel loves it! Lift roots with blow dryer, then break it up; or just spray eight to nine inches away all over. Controls without heaviness, and provides plenty of drama.

7 Mascara—never bat lashes without it!

8 Lip rouge for that just-kissed tint with a hint of gloss.

9 Highlighter pencil to glam it up at the eyebrow bone.

10 Face blotter to get rid of dirt and absorb unnecessary shine.

in the end

My best piece of beauty advice is to find a balance. A gorgeous gown can be bumped off best-dressed lists with the wrong hair and makeup. I've faced this on more than one occasion, despite the best of intentions. Several weeks of work to perfect a look—gown, jewelry, and shoes—can end up imploding if a hair stylist or makeup artist is more concerned with showing off his or her handiwork than the overall look and, even worse, the woman.

A helmet updo and too much eye *and* lip color can age even the prettiest gamine, and it definitely does no favors to women beyond that stage. I tend to consider an updo the death of almost any red carpet moment. I recall the time when I put a young client in a couture gown that should've summoned a very Sophia Loren effect. Instead, the severe updo turned her into a suburban bridesmaid.

five habits worth getting into

1. *A groomed brow can open up your eyes and frame your face. Tweeze a hair here or there between appointments, but see a professional at least every four to six weeks to maintain shape.*

2. *Whether you bleach, thread, or wax, get rid of any lip hair. A moustache is only handsome on men, and even then not in all cases.*

3. *Keep nails manicured, always. Even if that means a quickie, do-it-yourself removal of all polish traces, filing, and moisturizing. We all communicate with our hands, some more than others. Don't create distractions with badly chipped nails. Even worse are unloved feet—pedicure them or cover them up completely. The chicest nails, on fingers or toes, are trimmed at short length and polished in red, burgundy, natural, or clear.*

4. *Loofah skin. Along with shampooing, this should become part of your bathing ritual. Not only does it soften skin by sloughing away dead cells and environmental toxins, but it also opens pores, allowing for a closer shave or, later in the salon, better waxing.*

5. *Drink water. You'd think with all the bottle toting we do we'd be drowning in the stuff. But most of us (yours truly in particular) also do plenty of coffee drinking—and that zaps hydration. So does a night of bubbly. A good practice is to drink a tall glass while you do your makeup.*

Forget the updo and pull back hair into a simple, neat chignon that is forever chic and timeless . . .

...or instead opt for soft, relaxed hair to keep a glamour moment more modern.

My advice? Decide on hair and makeup only after choosing the dress. The aim is to juxtapose. If the dress is really serious, play down the makeup and pull back your hair into a loose chignon. A simpler look can warrant more of a statement with the hair and lips (or eyes—but never both). A no-frills, classic black sheath begs for more fun with beauty. Go sexy with tousled hair and a strong red lip. The goal is to play up the beauty or the outfit.

Don't go too period either or you risk looking dated. If you go with a 1960s-looking frock, stick to hair and makeup that don't turn you into an extra for a Richard Lester flick.

Let's be realistic. Most women dress for other women. But the men are looking at your face. Give them something they want to kiss. When in doubt, always remember: less is best. And don't forget, the best beauty mark of all is a generous smile.

chapter 6
behind closed doors

what happens style-wise behind closed doors, in your home, shouldn't just be incidental. Home isn't just where you stow your things or sack out for the night. It should be your private escape. It's a place where you want to bring friends to hang out. It doesn't need to be perfect, but it ought to be as close to perfect as you can make it.

Home should be where you live. Truly, completely live. It's no coincidence that lifestyle is the merging of life and style. Make your home the foundation of your lifestyle.

My life is so consumed with clutter—ideas, dresses, appointments, people. At any given moment in my studio, a room at the north end of my home, there can be a hundred dresses crammed on three racks, dozens and dozens of high heels carefully lined up in tight rows on the concrete floor, and mounds of jewelry and clutches and muffins and cookies sprawled on a six-foot table. Even though my assistants, relentlessly consummate as they are, keep the studio and my adjoining office as neat as possible, there's an endless clatter of phones, clients, their assistants, tailors, delivery men, flowers, and just plain stuff each day. Don't get me wrong, I love it. I thrive in it.

But this chaos is also the very reason why my home has to be a place that brings me peace and comfort. It has to be where I recharge and dream. As my career has flourished and I've grown up, it has become essential that home be a place that provides me with complete serenity and openness.

I can't emphasize this enough: regard your home—be it a dorm room, a temporary apartment, or a home you've lived in for decades—as an important area in your life. Invest in your environment, and not just in terms of money. Give it time. Give it meaningful consideration.

Luxury is creating, wholeheartedly, a den dedicated to intimacy, detail, and comfort. Glamour is divining a special retreat that is totally you.

point of view

When it comes to all parts of my life, I'm definitely visually oriented. Of all the senses, sight is the one that impacts me first and most sharply. It's what drove me to play dress-up as a child. Or to whittle away down time, perfectly content, people watching and filing one image after another away in my brain. I may not always remember names, but I remember an outfit. Obviously it has suited me well in my career as a stylist. But my home life is no exception.

No matter where I look inside my home, I like what I see.

This didn't just happen. So don't believe for a minute that you don't have it in you to reach this goal. Yet it does take one very jarring reality check: recognizing what it will take for you to skip out on an invitation because you can't dream of being anywhere else more delicious than home. This requires some research and patience to put it all together. Take out the camera and snap views of a room or corner. Study the images. You'll likely see something crying out for change—an out-of-place ugly cable or how the furniture is oddly lined up.

Making your true lifestyle part of your home is not a one-shot act, something you do when you move in and never revisit. It might even necessitate dedicating time each month, each season, to rearrange, refresh, and purge. In essence, creating your environment isn't unlike creating a wardrobe.

thinking outside the home

Just like finding the inspiration for your personal style, start imagining your interior style by considering what inspires you.

I'm always inspired by the hotels that become my home away from Los Angeles throughout the year. I love the pristine modernism. I love the way a good hotel allows its guests to shut out the world. How it makes life so easy, be it room service with special requests or another cozy throw to pull over the highest-thread count sheets. There is also something very practical about a hotel room, with a place for everything. In New York, I'm a constant presence at 60 Thompson, and I love St. Martins Lane in London. Both feel like home.

Not all of my favorites are temples to minimalism either. I can find inspiration in the dramatic eclecticism that fills the Viceroy Hotels under

Rodger and I bought our first house, we began by considering what had made us happy at our previous residences, what we liked in the many, many hotels we have checked into year-round, and what we found memorable or motivating in homes we had visited through our lives.

Even if you've never been in a place or met a person that inspires you, you can still have an emotional or aesthetic reaction that allows you to dream up your own version. The first step in decorating a home involves assembling magazine tears, snapshots, memories, paint chips, and fabric swatches. These could even be images of a dress or a garden that evoke a shade or vibe you want in your home. Jam them in a folder that you'll keep in your bag or your car as a reference and a reminder of your direction.

Modern doesn't have to mean stark minimalism.

Kelly Wearstler's keen sense of style. And even though the décor is miles from my modernist sensibility, I always stay at the elegantly old-school Hôtel Costes on rue St-Honoré in Paris for the very reason that the staff is so well-dressed and the courtyard is the most fantastic place for us to gather and gossip during fashion week. The people-watching alone is a visual feast. Other favorite grand ol' hotels are the Plaza Athénée (near all the good shopping on Avenue Montaigne) in Paris and the florid Dorchester near London's Hyde Park. The vases crammed with freshly cut flowers and the general calmness throughout make these secondary addresses welcome respites from my long workdays in those cities.

So why shouldn't the elements I love about my favorite hotels come home with me? In 2004, when

Your home is an extension of you. So is it a surprise that my house is awash in whites and neutrals? For some visitors, it is. Take away the piles of gold chains and cuffs, the platform stilettos, and the baroque bags made of color-saturated lizard skins and you'll find my favorite dresses are really very spare and direct. Consider my point of view—a kind of bohemian glamour rooted in modernism. There is a late 1960s and 1970s sensibility to the way I dress. And so, too, in the way I've styled my home. It's why I adore Halston so much. He understood that modern doesn't have to mean stark minimalism. Today's equivalent would be Tom Ford, of course, who still manages to inject a flourish of glamour into his environments.

The shades of white on the walls and furnishings, along with walls and furnishings of glass,

home *sexy* home

*I love snakes, especially gold ones. No one loves them as much, and perhaps even more than me, as **Roberto Cavalli**. They are, of course, only one of the key motifs that are signature throughout his collections, his stores, and his homes—all of which epitomize sexiness, extravagance, and glamour. We also share an untamed penchant for all things leopard, fur, gold, and lavish. Roberto and I go way back to my days of dressing the boy bands, and I continue to dress my clients, and myself, in his clothes and jewelry. I also love his gorgeous wife and business partner Eva Duringer, an Austrian beauty he met as a judge in the Miss Universe pageant. Don't you love that? They have three children together (in addition to his two other children) and continue to rock their empire, their parties, and their three homes in high style. Here Roberto explains why home may be one of the most significant reflections of your lifestyle and you.*

Living among beautiful things is therapeutic. It transmits energy, strength, and harmony. It is essential for someone who is always looking for new inspirations to create beauty.

Roberto Cavalli

Home represents the contraposition to work's stressful and frantic rhythms. Living in places surrounded with beauty, art, and culture can have the same value that family, love, and friendship have to reinvigorate ourselves and fill our souls. We Italians have a sense of glamour like few others because of our joy and enthusiasm for everything.

In my opinion, the key features of a house are determined by the place in which it is located and by the role it plays. I have three houses located in different places and playing different roles, which, even though they greatly differ, reflect the multiple traits of my personality.

My house in Florence, where I have always lived with my family and where my deepest roots are, is the most important one. It is a tower built in the eleventh century on top of a hill, overlooking the city and the Florentine countryside. I love this house especially because it is where my children grew up. It is full of warmth, voices, and memories. Everything has a history there. I can produce my own wine, collect unique Tuscan artwork, play in the park with my beloved animals, and, above all, devote myself completely to my family and friends. My house is always open.

The Milan house is the one I use mainly for work. It is a spectacular open loft full of light and decorated with contemporary artwork that I am particularly fond of, such as my portrait by Julian Schnabel, a zebra armchair (a gift from my wife), an original sculpture of a Persian horse from 1500, antique Chinese ceramics, many photos, big spheres, and other objects. What I like about this house is the idea that a bright white space is colored with Roberto Cavalli's world, with my big works of art, design, and colorful objects.

In New York, I live in a small alcove in the middle of the Big Apple's chaos, with big windows offering a breathtaking view of Central Park. This is my shelter where I love to play with all my electronics. It's a very energetic place, completely opposite from the peace of the Florentine hills.

Even if you only have a single residence, there are certainly ways to personalize it with elements reflecting your lifestyle. The secret is choosing the paintings, fabrics, light effects, and collected objects that best represent the memory of a trip, a happy moment, or an unforgettable vacation. All of this makes a house warm and cozy and communicates its history—and your own.

Making a home sexy comes down to choosing fabrics and materials that are pleasant to touch: silk rugs, taffeta curtains, leather couches, and wooden floors. Then there's the choice of lighting: nothing is sexier than light to warm up the ambience, loosen it up, and make it feel like your house.

bolster the general airiness of our home. An all-white contemporary environ can be cold and clinical, but it is warmed up with dark woods—like the deep, rich planks on the floors, and thick, varnished frames on the sliding doors—which creates a kind of sensuality to the space. If you can't change your floors and doors, introduce warmer wood furnishings, like a beautiful chair or a set of smoothly wrought African bowls.

somebody lives here

Humanizing a space is something many style junkies forget to do. This isn't an exclusive problem among modernism lovers. Even a salon filled with antiques can feel like a museum.

Humanizing a space doesn't necessarily mean cluttering up the place with photographs of family and friends. I prefer to keep my memories in albums, because desktop frames filled with smiling poses always remind me of an office. Which is, by the way, why the desk in my office is the only place in my house where you'll find them.

Make as many areas of your home inviting by creating conversational zones. To do this, there has to be seating. I know this sounds obvious. But think of all the times you were left leaning against an arm of furniture that's also facing a television. Create a quasi-circle, where collectives of guests, or even all of you living under the same roof, can gather. While you're at it, give every seat in the house a view—whether it's a picture on a wall, an open window, or a rare orchid in a corner.

About that television. A room with the focus centered on a TV is a conversation flow killer. Even if the TV is not on. Since it's likely your home is like mine and there does happen to be a TV in a common space or two, there are ways around this. Keep it covered. We have one set inside a cabinet, sitting behind closed doors almost all the time. That isn't an option for another of our TVs, a flat-screen hanging exposed on the wall. If that's your

home, too, then when it comes time to entertaining, position a chair or two in front of the screen so it becomes part of the conversation zone.

Too often contemporary means a blindingly chilly amount of shiny and burnished metal. I say stainless steel in moderation. A ribbon of it frames the oversized pair of mirrors in our breakfast area. Highly polished, curved legs fabulously counter the white, textured ostrich skin of a rocking chair in our media lounge. And there's no defending the beautifully bold statement of the Arco Lamp, which stands ever proudly in that same room.

A good way to soften the edges is healthy green plants. I did say healthy. Dead anything inside a house is dead energy. Lush green plants and blooming flowers bring nature indoors, and can be so elegant. I'm partial to tropical varieties like mini palms and orchids, with their full green leaves.

Create a communal area that is well lit. An oversized mirror— this one leans against the wall—instantly boosts light and space.

for keeps

Most furniture can be a costly proposition. But if you can hold out for pieces, even a few, that hold their value and that you love, then it's an investment worth making. Even when it comes to finally letting go of a beloved piece, because you're moving or redecorating, a quality piece can usually be resold again. It's something Rodger and I have thought about with each home.

The Arco Lamp is one of three major pieces we brought with us to L.A. The 1962 design of white marble and slim stainless steel seems to be bending from the weight of its shiny bulbous head. I can't help but marvel daily at its ultra sleek style. It was a big-ticket buy in the first place. Dragging the 160-pound lamp across country only increased our outlay. But if (and that's a big if) we ever do decide to get rid of it, it will likely sell for at least what we paid. Inspirational as it is to look at, it's also an investment.

The same goes for two other pieces we hauled out from Manhattan. One of the first major pieces we bought together was a Philippe Starck couch. We collapse into this deep box, which is more like a bed, when we stay home for the evening to sneak in a movie. Covered in bright white cotton, it's like our little cloud on which to float away from reality. It's insanely comfortable. There is always a colorful cashmere blanket or two folded over the high arms, which we invariably reach for. Nearby, against the wall, is a wooden Christian Liaigre bench. It's funny that the Starck sofa, Arco lamp, and Liaigre bench all ended up in the same room where Rodger and I tend to go to decompress.

In our current home in L.A., a major investment was our white leather B&B Italia sofa. It epitomizes the very laid-back, chic, and modern lifestyle I wanted to communicate with our home. I searched everywhere for a comparable, less pricey alternative. But I always loved this particular sofa. My parents moved theirs from house to house over three decades. They'll never get rid of it. I couldn't imagine living without ours.

Even with limited resources, you don't have to completely compromise your dreams. You *can* do better. Cheap stuff can look worse with wear. Also, resist the

cable free

There are very few instances in fashion where a garment's constructional foundation and everything else holding a body together under a dress needs to be seen. Do you really want to catch an unintended peek of a thigh-skimming slimmer? The same goes for all those electrical wires snaking around exposed throughout the house. Don't let electronics show. If they must, make sure they deserve the exposure. Store appliances when they're not in use, even in the kitchen. Go wireless or compact whenever possible. If a TV has to show (and it does in our home), minimize its presence. Tuck away everything else involved in a media center. Hide the mechanisms or any other workings of your home. Or at least ensure they look good—even if that means a bit of camouflage courtesy of a sculpture or pot.

urge to blow your small bundle on pieces you think are temporary, or it's very likely you'll find yourself comfortably living among them well past their expiration date.

To do better might involve a bit more adventure and tenacity than popping into your local mall. There are great modern pieces to be had at irresistible deals on eBay and Craigslist, as well as in vintage stores catering to the era. Legions of young modern designers are also creating fabulous pieces at accessible prices that are being sold at boutiques and online. You can usually learn about them in the shelter section of your newspaper or on design blogs such as apartmenttherapy.com or designsponge.blogspot.com. Think of it this way: supporting such fledgling talent is not only good for your pocketbook, it also enables you to be a kind of patron of the craft.

light bright

Tear down the drapes. Take a hammer to a wall. Do whatever it takes to let the sun shine in.

Natural light is invigorating. Give me the sun any day over artificial lighting. That's why I needed a place with plenty of windows. I like seeing out. I love being close to the outdoors. Not in a granola girl kind of way, of course. That's so not me. But I connect absolutely to the ideal of "California living" and all that it suggests—open views, breezes, and sunlight. I think that's part of why I needed to leave New York, as much as I truly love the charge I get from that city. Living under the shadows of those tall buildings, I felt a sense of claustrophobia. I always craved the endless tree-filled, sun-soaked landscape of my younger years in Short Hills.

Wide glass windows—walls, really—define much of my home, a mid-century, single-level home that Rodger and I overhauled and updated before moving in. Glass walls that make up a southern corner provide a postcard view of L.A., complete with palm trees—a perfect setting for our long white dining table and chairs. We stuck sliding doors in the living room area and bedroom, and the behemoth front door is also crystal clear.

Our escape zone, utterly comfortable with a cashmere blanket at reach, plenty of pillows, and the Arco lamp overhead for reading

A view is a view. Make the best of it. Just direct that natural light in however you can. If you really can't bear seeing the landscape beyond your window, position a tall, leafy plant in front of it or hang a super-sheer cotton curtain (there are exceptions to my declarations, of course), which will still allow light to filter through.

Artificial light can't be avoided, but it can be upgraded into something less harsh. We went with several Plexiglas and glass fixtures in our place, including a Giogali chandelier, this cluster of chain-link Murano glass, hanging in our foyer. Those pieces give maximum luminosity without being blinding. If you do consider a glass globe or similar light covering, go with a bulb that is under sixty watts. Another terrific option is going with tinted or milky glass or Plexi shades. I'm not recommending you do your entire home this way, but a table lamp or pendant light here and there in these materials can look both modern and chic.

Don't underestimate the power of a great little lamp or a grouping of candles either. There are all kinds of sculptural, spare lamps that can make an engaging statement on a table or desk, or even on the floor. Candles can certainly create a mood and perk up another of the senses if they're scented. Neither option has to dent the plastic, and they can be among the accents you switch out from year to year when the place needs a pick-me-up.

making a statement

It's the accessories that really count. They do when you're styling yourself and they are just as key when it comes to styling your living space.

Like the dress, furniture should be subtly chic. Accentuate with sexy colors, artful objects, and any other ornamentation that reveals you. Ask yourself, does this color or texture make me feel beautiful? If so, indulge. Pottery, bedding, dishes, and even flowers can completely refresh a space—and your mood.

I tend to dress up my house like I do myself: in bold, statement-making accessories. I typically reserve a shot of color for my purse or lips, and so I prefer to reserve it for the items decorating a blonde table or punching up a white leather bench. A staple category in my wardrobe is fur—real, fake, shrugs, and coats. A great square fur throw covers our bed. Consider a plush faux pelt on the floor at the foot of the bed or over a favorite reading chair.

I may be a bit promiscuous when it comes to designers in my wardrobe. But for home, it's pretty

Create a welcoming entrance with fresh flowers, loved artwork (as in this Adam Harteau lithograph of Kate Moss), and books.

clear I have a thing for Missoni. Their signature multicolors zigzag my oversized pool towels, the bedspreads in both bedrooms, the throw pillows, and the dishes. They're the perfect punctuation in our white house.

Create new ways of showcasing things you love. The oversized coffee table we chose has a deep open-sided well where I can show off my many fashion books, some cherished vintage tomes I received as gifts over the years. Among my faves is a 1967 first-edition copy of *Harper's Bazaar: 100 Years of the American Female*, which Glenda Bailey, the editor in chief of Bazaar and a huge support to me, gave me for my birthday. Conventional bookcases are not really my thing, so neat stacks of books also appear around the house. But only display books that you really love and enjoy. Nothing is more pretentious than stacks of books that are meaningless to you but are there just for looks.

I collect antique *Vogue* covers, and have many dating back to the 1930s. Those were the days when magazine cover art was a painting or drawing. I've framed several favorites and grouped them on a wall in my office. You can find all kinds of amazing art in old magazines at flea markets and used bookstores, even through dealers that specialize in them.

a touch of *luxe*

Even a small living space can have a big sense of modern luxury with a few touches:

- White walls are a clean, modern backdrop and reflect natural light, which is important to the mood of a room and the mood of the people in it. (I'm just that much more happy in a room filled with natural light.)

- Less is more. Dress walls, tables, and other surfaces with fewer objects. There's nothing modern about a cluttered space. Your cherished pieces will look as luxurious as they are with room to breathe.

- Cashmere or lambs wool throws provide instant richness and are completely yummy to get under.

- Pillows covered in fur, real or faux, are a sexy addition to any room.

- Candles scented with fig, tuberose, amber, Madagascar, or some other indulgent essence can instantly shift your mood. Light them as soon as you get home, even for no reason than you're just home.

- A great chair that makes a statement on its own is a great anchor to a room. It doesn't have to be something oversized and loud. Even a simple, completely Plexiglas clear dining chair standing away from the corner can have impact.

Group your favorite photography books . . .

. . . or collectible magazine covers.

Art, of course, is much more than mere accessory. But like every choice in your home, there should be an intimate correlation with its very presence on your walls. My parents are avid collectors of contemporary works, and they particularly love treasure hunting fledgling talent before they become the flavor of the moment (and their prices skyrocket!). They've been angels to my fledgling collection, too, gifting me with several great pieces for my home.

Even if you think you know nothing about art, you most certainly can recognize what you like, right? You also don't have to have a trust fund to collect. Start with an inexpensive print and get it beautifully framed. It can be a favorite musician or stage performer—as long as it's an image with a lot of style. Then be willing to graduate to a photographer or painter you uncover at a local gallery, or even online. Archives like those from the *New York Times* and the Los Angeles Public Library offer a gold mine of iconic photographs for just a couple of hundred bucks. It's amazing.

Even a single, favorite work can impact a room—and your life. I can't help but smile every time I look at my photograph of Twiggy, a small, colorful portrait that hangs near the kitchen entrance. I love portraits. I have the sexiest black-and-white Johnny Depp image shot by Nigel Perry in the living room. And for my thirty-fifth birthday, my sister got me the four individual solarized portraits of the Beatles that Richard Avedon took in 1966. Love her!

If you're just starting out, buy a softback edition of a book by William Claxton, Mick Rock, or Irving Penn and carefully slice out the pages and frame them. Or get a dozen postcards of great images and frame them individually in simple black or metal frames. Then hang them together. Great photography is great photography, whether it's an autographed print or not.

Don't forget to inject a little fun into your choice of accessories, too. Rose loves to wear a broach of an emerald green beetle—a once live and kicking beetle!—with gold wire legs. She keeps it pinned to her black wool Vivienne Westwood coat, so it's perfect. It's also very funny. Extend that sense of humor to your home. For a recent birthday, my agent and friend gave me a set of silver and leather-handled gardening tools from Hermès. I'm obsessed with Hermès accessories, but I do not garden. My agent does. So the set makes me smile every time I catch sight of it—on my fireplace mantel!

Unlike heavy furniture that might require a strong man to help move, interior accessories can be relocated or switched out in a snap. If your taste changes with a season or other influence, a blanket in the latest color or dishes in a brand-new pattern can easily freshen up the place.

If an artist print is not an option, frame a copy of a favorite black-and-white photograph.

a few of my *favorite frills*

Colorful Missoni blankets

The Arco Lamp by Achille & Pier Giacomo Castiglioni

Vintage *Vogue* magazine covers, framed and grouped

Various artworks featuring Johnny Depp, including a Nigel Perry black-and-white portrait

Collection of Visionaire editions and toys

live and in technicolor: margherita missoni

I'm mad for Missoni. I live in their caftans and on their bed covers. But it's the family I really adore. As the third generation of the vibrantly colored fashion house her grandparents, Rosita and Tai Missoni, created, young Margherita Maccapani Missoni is a great friend who always makes sure we have a lavish time in whatever city we find ourselves in. So, too, her beautiful mother, Angela, who heads design for the women's line.

Months after moving into her very first apartment, a Manhattan flat a continent away from Milan, Margherita found out that she had a week to polish off her decorating dreams: three magazines wanted to showcase the aspiring actress's new digs, and a fourth shoot involved her campaign as the face of her family's signature fragrance for Esteé Lauder. This girl's got amazing taste, and she pulled off the decorating in the same fanciful nonchalance that epitomizes her personal style. Margherita shares her way.

Even though I had to complete my apartment rather quickly, I already had plenty to work with and so it was just a matter of finally making the time to wrap it up. We get so busy with our lives. But, if I can advise anything, it's *make the time.*

I decorate like I dress. Never too matchy. I'm not a very organized person, so even if I wanted a white minimalist home like Rachel's, I'd probably end up with what I have now. It's me. I love to mix colors, textures, and periods. I find a lot in flea markets. Here in New York, I found a 1950s dining table with a yellow Formica top and a leaf design in the metal frame, and these little tables covered in mosaic that I use collectively as a coffee table. I bought all these cheap colored vases and filled them in a 1920s glass vitrine that I also got there. My mom always said you can never have too many different-sized vases, and she's right. They add instant color even without flowers.

I always approach the flea market by not looking for anything specifically. When I do, I never find it. By being open to anything it's like things find me: above my sofa I have a patchwork of bunnies and deer, and a set of real antlers. Other than color, the forest motif helps tie it all together. I also collect drinking glasses from flea markets, some printed with colorful patterns or woodland animals.

I love buying stuff from around the world. I have two heart-shaped mirrors and a very old statue that I bought in Bali on a recent summer holiday. They remind me of my time there. Much of what I have in my home has meaning.

I use personal accessories to decorate. Around a 1960s Plexiglas and mirror vanity next to my bed, I hammered all of these nails to hang my large collection of necklaces. I didn't have a headboard, so on the wall I nailed loads of colorfully painted tin ornaments, like skulls and crosses, from Mexico. They remind me of little charms. They're very cheap but have a lot of impact. My mom puts them on the Christmas tree, so they also remind me of her.

Art is also very much a part of my surroundings, and years ago my mom started giving us a work by a rising artist each Christmas. They are quite affordable when she gets them, the same price as a good pair of shoes. Some of them have even gone up in value over the years! Even if you don't have a lot in your house, some artwork can dress up the place. But it has to be something you will like looking at every day. That alone makes it a good investment. Don't hang something you don't care about. Or you're better off hanging an old frame with nothing in it.

I feel more at home in color. Of course, I have tons of Missoni pillows everywhere. They provide comfort and color. But they also help tie in the different colors featured in each room. My bedroom is in pinks and Bordeaux, and the living room is in browns and greens. Even the bathroom, which is very tiny, is like a rainbow. I have colored ribbons hanging from the ceiling, and on them I pin my broaches and earrings. I also mix my dishes—patterns and stripes, black and white with colors.

You know, my family always made fun of me, teasing that I was the only one who didn't cook. But I'm now really good at risotto, pasta, scallopini. When you finally make a home you love, you start doing things you never imagined.

Pillow talk: Margarita and me.

private parts

Home might be a retreat of peace and comfort even for those friends and family we love, but the bedroom is a haven with a do-not-disturb sign.

Next to time, sleep is luxury. I don't get enough of it. I'm sure you don't get enough of it either. Long workdays that can stretch into the night and a demanding social calendar can mean being too beyond exhausted sometimes to even care if the sheet thread count is 300 or more. But it does matter. Okay, so maybe you won't have the same set of sheets forever, but high-quality linens with a 300 count or higher of Egyptian cotton do last longest—and feel best. Definitely a good investment.

Whether you live alone or with a lover, the bedroom should be about the bed. There shouldn't be anything that reminds you about work (including an office in the corner) or socializing. Keep the photos from the family holiday and a friend's birthday in the other rooms. Keep the environment pared down and sensual. Remove any books that you are not currently reading. Stow away anything that belongs in the closet or drawers. Sensuality is about the senses, so think accordingly: scented candles, the right temperature, pleasing textures. On Rodger's and my bed, the combination of knit Missoni pillows and the soft fur throw makes it as cozy as a favorite sweater and fur coat pairing.

Modern doesn't have to mean minimal. A fur throw and Missoni knit pillows create a sensual texture in the bedroom. Light scented candles whenever you spend any time in a room.

out of sight

Just as a kitchen looks better with appliances stored away (or as many as possible), keep the exhibition of personal care products to a minimum. Showing off to your loved ones just how many bottles of moisturizer and compacts of eye shadow you've amassed by leaving them all out for them to see is just not that interesting. Put it away. If it doesn't all fit in the bathroom, then find another place to keep products, organized and updated. The bathroom is a place to get clean. Keep it looking that way, too.

closet case

I've probably been the luckiest clotheshorse in the world, and not necessarily for the reasons you might think. I always manage to find a home with a roomy walk-in closet, one that *should* contain my world. It never does. Partly to blame are my organizational skills when it comes to clothes and accessories.

I admit it! My glamour trappings runneth over. It's a challenge to keep everything in its place when life is in overtime. But what eases the process is having a place for everything. My mother is a master at this. I suppose she has to be, to contain the tons and tons of jewelry, real and costume, that she has collected during her lifetime. She could fill several coffee-table volumes with her collections from individual designers. It's incredible. Her treasury is truly Shangri-La.

Her system isn't the fanciest, but it is the most practical and effective. It's also one of the only reasons you'd ever spot my mother at a DIY store. She's not exactly handy with the hammer. The sectional boxes used to organize screws and nails are perfectly suited to organize the nuts and bolts of a girl's own wardrobe. Line them with swatches of fabric to protect pieces that are more delicate. The clear tops allow for quick surveying. The hard plastic keeps everything protected. They stack. They're easily portable. They're cheap. They're really pretty perfect.

My dream has always been to have custom built-

Shangri-La!

Dream drawers

in jewelry drawers in my closet, and I made sure they were part of the plans when we overhauled my house. Even a closet case on a budget can realize this with a free-standing dresser or cabinet that can be positioned inside a closet or in the corner of a room. A good-looking option is a horizontal plan chest, the super-strength steel units with skinny drawers used to store blueprints. They're usually lockable, which is a plus.

As my built-in drawers are already starting to overflow a bit, those sectional boxes are proving, again, rather handy.

sorting it all out

While I may have inherited my mother's proclivity for jewelry and accessories, my sister Pamela scored her organizational skills. So I'll let the master take it from here:

Rachel and our mom are very similar when it comes to their closets. They have an abundance of amazing, really quality pieces. They also have so much that if it's not organized, they can't see what they have. Lucky for them, I love to organize it all when I visit.

The end goal here is to know what you have and where to find it. It's also the starting point. Lay out everything you have. In the case of jewelry, that's every pendant, stud, ring—everything. With Rachel's trove, when floor and counter space in the bathroom and bedroom are completely filled, we invade the hallway and keep going until everything is spread out. This same exercise should be applied to clothes, handbags, and footwear. Really, anything contained in your closet and drawers.

Next is "editing"—a more diplomatic term than "throwing out." Some editing takes place as we lay out everything. Obvious why-do-I-still-have-these items don't even hit the floor. But the real task is in the concerted editing. This is where it helps having a friend—or sister—who will ask the hard questions:

- *When was the last time you wore this?*

- *Why are you holding on to this?*

- *Will you ever wear it again?*

- *Do you love it?*

Organize by color or style.

Now this is very important: as soon as a bauble or blouse is nixed, put it out of sight. Immediately. Otherwise, nostalgia or some other emotion will inevitably creep in and nothing will get edited it out.

Like Rachel said, the sectional hardware cases are a great solution, with everything separated by category or style—gold, silver, crystal, costume, day, evening. (I have filled container upon container for these two.) Shoeboxes can work, too. Just be sure to label them so each box can be accessed quickly when you've only got ten minutes to get your glamour on for the night. (I remember doing this exercise with Rachel a few years ago and Bakelite bangles filled an entire boot box!)

Organize the rest of the closet with an eye toward harmony. It could be category or color, but aim for a presentation that makes you smile every time you face your closet. Or at least doesn't cause you to freak out over where everything is.

Sort out handbags by category—oversized, clutch, day, bijoux, and so on. That said, Rachel makes an exception with her collection of Chanel bags, which she groups together regardless of style or color.

Shoes look and work particularly well lined up by color, then suborganized by heel type. If you have the space, bookshelves are a great way to organize them. If you don't, hanging shoe storage bags and clear plastic boxes are fine for footwear, bags, and other accessories. What's important is that everything has a place.

On the rack, hang clothes according to category first, then color. Even the smallest of wardrobes looks best this way. If you can trade out plastic hangers for wood, do. Or at least go with the same color or kind for a consistent appearance.

The edit is particularly important with clothes. Weed out anything that no longer fits well or no longer excites you. If it still has the tags on it because you bought it, hung it, and forgot it, then get rid of it. And if you definitely wouldn't want to get caught in public in it, toss it out.

ultimately

You have to hold on to what gets you going. If you haven't used it, or you haven't known it's been buried in the back of the cabinet or closet for three years, then let it go. Never, ever get rid of photos, or your first loves. But if you have something that you know is an eyesore, get rid of it. If it doesn't work in your life anymore, get rid of it. If it's not making you smile, or inspiring you, get rid of it.

Every day that I walk into my house, I love my house. Love where you live.

the fearless five: a questionable matter

you don't love something, let it go. That's easier said than done, I know. Even something invested with memories doesn't have to take up valuable space forever. Store it or let someone else create a memory with it. Having trouble making a clean sweep? Ask yourself:

1   Why am I holding on to it?

2   Is it worth anything?

3   What kind of shape is it in, and is it beyond repair?

4   Can I replace it?

5   Do I want to replace it with an updated version?

chapter 7
entertaining

entertaining by definition is about diversion, amusement, pleasure. Despite the controlling Virgo within me when it comes to work, I can never understand why a party would turn into anxiety and hard labor for the person throwing it. It's precisely because of the overwrought schedules and unsympathetic deadlines that define our modern lives that I don't spend a heck of a lot of time planning out a dinner party at home or drinks at a favorite hangout. Life is manic enough as it is with work and chores and other prosaic responsibilities that the very opportunity to entertain is a delicious indulgence I dream about. So in order to make it happen I just put the call out and do it.

For yours truly, entertaining is a democratic proposition: fun for one and all—and that includes the host.

from time to time

The type of invitation you send out depends entirely on the event. If it's a last-minute or more casual gathering, a phone call or even an e-mail message is perfectly fine. If it's a special event, say, a birthday or anniversary, send an announcement by snail mail. Nothing beats the arrival in the mail of beautiful stationery—the way the quality and texture of the paper feel to the touch is a thrill.

There are so many options these days. Custom letterpresses are popping up around the country, and there are ready-made boxes of letterpress and handcrafted cards available at better card and gift stores. A truly life-marking event like an engagement or the birth of a child might warrant custom-printed cards, and these can be created at home if you're handy with a computer (which I admittedly am not) or at a local card shop or printer. Even a handwritten note does the trick. The aim here is to convey how much you care about this occasion in your life, and how much you'd like your guests to share it with you.

Even the circus of haute couture week in Paris requires a little break with friends. A late-night supper interlude at my fave l'Avenue with my talented designing pals Giambattista Valli and Erin Fetherston.

If you're on the receiving end of the invite, an RSVP is not optional. Don't overlook how important it is to your host that you reply within the requested time. If it's your event, don't stalk guests about coming. Follow up once. If they don't call, they're either avoiding you or dead.

Check in advance the availability of any friends whose presence is really important to the event. Believe me, I've made the mistake of not checking first and ended up doing twice the work to accomodate someone who I really wanted to attend.

With my dear Tamara

Setting the time for a party is crucial to providing cues—or confusion—among your guests. For a cocktail hour, give a start and finish time, say 7 to 10 P.M., even if the party runs much later. Otherwise dinner will be expected.

If there's dinner involved, then a true cocktail hour preceding the meal can begin around seven, too. Provide appetizers for those inevitably starving pals, but keep the starters light. They should whet appetites and keep your famished friends from getting prematurely sauced. Serve dinner an hour or so later, followed by dessert, conversation, and plenty of laughs.

**Carine Roitfeld and
Natalia Vodianova**

In general, indicate an end time, some thirty minutes before you actually want it to end. Leave it as a question mark, if you prefer, but be ready to go the distance. Sneaking off to bed at your own affair is not an option for a host famously known among her friends for living it up.

The invite should always list a complete address of the location since many now rely on Mapquest and other online locators to find their way. Don't overlook the parking. If your budget allows for valet, then hire a respectable firm. If not, provide parking suggestions in the invitation. Many neighborhoods require parking permits after certain hours, so have plenty on hand, inform your guests that they're available, and keep them near the front door.

**Francisco Costa
of Calvin Klein**

food for thought

While I like to cook, I personally don't like cooking for a party. I've learned I can't enjoy the company I've invited over if I'm so worried about the timing of the meal. It's better to recognize your limits and build on your strengths, right? If you like to cook for a party and can manage to play host, more power to you. Give yourself plenty of time, especially to look your best when the first guest arrives.

But me? I don't like to be a working host when I could be relaxed and giving my guests my undivided attention.

When Rodger and I christened our new home with a party for my parents, we made sure it would be as much fun for us as it would be for everyone there. My mom and dad were in town to see our place for the first time, and since so many of our friends had never met them, we called it "Meet the Parents" night.

A good host never regrets having too much to eat on hand, yet always frets if it runs out too soon. If I invite ten guests, I order for fifteen. The menu should have options in appetizers and entrees, because you never know what your guests' current dietary needs are. I'm a vegetarian and allergic to wheat, yet I never want to stress the host out about it. I always keep that in mind when I'm throwing the party.

Don't forget the champagne!

I called in a tasty spread from my favorite gourmet deli, Joan's on Third, which sells all kinds of cheeses, meats, and condiments from France and Italy. Plus, the cooks there concoct the best ready-to-chow foods. We had plenty to drink and eat through the evening at self-service tables crammed with bottles and platters.

Our friends lingered late, and my parents, Rodger, and I had the most freewheeling time. Just because a party's catered doesn't mean it should feel formal. When I invite people to my home, it's to chill. I don't want them to feel they have to show up buttoned-up and eat tiny bits of food.

The same goes with the bar. Have nonalcoholic options, of course. But don't limit the liquor choices to one. Some guests might hate the taste or effects of gin, while others may be sensitive to the sulfites in red wine. Don't forget the champagne either!

Dessert is essential. I always offer something chocolate and something ice cream. I don't like to go too fancy with dessert. A great fruit cobbler, fruit and cheese, or a mixed cookie plate can satisfy plenty a sweet tooth. Have teas and coffee, unleaded and regular.

Be it drink or eats, know your crowd.

setting the stage at home

Whether you're thrilled with your home decor or not, a bunch of flowers, candles, and dim lighting can put everyone in the right mood. Go with any flowers in season. My personal favorites are anything white, such as calla lilies, orchids, peonies, or white tulips in big bunches. I like my candles white, too, although, depending on the season, black or garnet shades can also strike a beautiful effect. In candles or flowers, beware of a mishmash of colors and scents. You don't want to clutter your home or everyone's senses with too much of anything.

If place and weather permit, stretch the scene outdoors. The candles and flowers can thread through the two spaces, while the change in atmosphere can boost the party energy. It's particularly ideal, too, should any guests smoke.

Soirées taking place completely outdoors require a bit more consideration. Be it the beach or a park, bring enough blankets and, if daytime hours are involved, sunscreen to share. Secure any necessary permits in advance (never assume you won't need them).

Watch the weather report in the days leading up to the bash. If it's really windy, just cancel and reschedule. And consider a menu that's not too messy. There is nothing sensuous about sand on barbecue-sauce-tipped fingers.

For house parties, I love a buffet. It depends on the crowd, of course, but the advantage of a buffet is that guests eat when they're hungry and can go back for seconds a fourth time. It allows them to move freely and gab with whoever they want (well, just about). And that promotes an easier, more relaxed environment.

Like the food, seating should be plentiful. Even if it's throw pillows and blankets on the floor, which can imbue a carefree cool to an event. Guests should always feel they have a place to sit.

If it's a seated affair, keep the table layout focused. Place cards can be great because they do away with those awkward moments of everyone wondering where they should sit. It also allows you to mix and match guests according to any grand plans you may have for them in terms of business, friendship, even romance.

Dinnerware can be quite an investment, so consider a set that can service a range of circumstances. I like the drama of an oversized dinner plate (a penchant inherited from my mom, who adores entertaining). I also love a modern setting, and in my case that means everything silver or white, down to our the platinum-rimmed white bone china. (I do have a colorful Missoni collection on special order, however!)

out of bounds

For all the benefits of entertaining at home, sometimes I just want to get out of the house. Maybe the place isn't sparkling, or the bar and fridge are in desperate need of restocking. These are no reasons to altogether nix a chance to celebrate.

At these moments, sanctuary and service are available at a nearby restaurant, bar, or nightclub. Some of my most intimate and rollicking memories with friends have taken place in very public venues thanks to a bit of advance planning and the comfort of the place.

amy sacco
on the home bar

The perfect host is always ready for an impromptu cocktail party. I know this all too well at Bungalow 8, where all kinds of friends show up at all kinds of hours ready to have the time of their lives. As the owner, I have to ensure that they feel right at home. At your place, having the following essentials in stock will make your personal bungalow just as great.

The Tools

Corkscrew: a cheapie with a fold-out knife for slicing off the foil on bottle tops is fine.

Double jigger: to measure liquid.

Shaker: make sure the top fits securely before use.

Cocktail spoon: a long, slim spoon for gently stirring drinks.

Glasses

Old-fashioned glasses—those squat, short ones—are a good way to go. Use them for cocktails or wine. (I love the small colored Moroccan glasses and you can get them cheap by the case.)

Bottle Service

Vodka

Bourbon

Rum (light is the most versatile)

Tequila

Gin

Whiskey (blended is the most mixable)

Beer

Wine (keep a couple of bottles of white always chilled)

Champagne (like the white, always have it ready to go)

Sodas and a juice or two to mix (white cranberry is oh-so chic)

The Extras

Brown sugar (for mojitos)

Lemons and limes

Life is on fast mode so much of the time that it's nice to be able to have a friend (or more) over for an impromptu drink (or more). Having everything in place before asking, "What are you having?" makes the process much more pleasurable. Be sure to wipe down the rims of the bottles and all the tools before stowing them away. Open wine should be thrown out after a couple of days (a vacuum cap can keep it for a day or two more, but not longer). Have plenty of ice on hand. Cheers.

Amy Sacco

My living room away from home at the Chateau Marmont in Hollywood

The Chateau Marmont on the Sunset Strip is just such a home away from home in my little book, where I always feel utterly relaxed, nestled into the velvety, beat-up lounge or outdoors in the social gardens. Part of the reason I moved to California was to experience life outdoors, and there's nothing quite like reclining in one of the rattan chairs under the moonlight. The Chateau has a quality which *j'adore* while I'm there, despite my madness for everything modern in my real life.

It's always good to have a favorite haunt with history, and this place has it in spades. It was built in 1929—making it very ancient property in L.A.—modeled after the Chateau Amboise in France's Loire Valley.

Helmut Newton met his mortal end there in 2004, but I suppose the best-known guest who passed on there was John Belushi. Because it's a home away from home for actors, fashion designers, and rock stars alike, the Chateau's new owner, my friend André Balazs, and his staff are vigilant about keeping tabloid eyes out. Even though there are times throughout the year when I spend hours cooped up in an upstairs suite or in a bungalow, in fittings with one star or another, I know that steps away there's a couch or dinner table with my name on it.

I love that it is a somewhat exclusive place, so it never gets too crowded. Take that into account when planning something off-site: a private room or an area that feels separate from the rest of the place can make all the difference if you're entertaining outside of your home. Another plus about the Chateau is the staff. They take care of everything in the most charming manner. Whatever place you decide on for a party, be sure that the service treats its guests well. Talk to your point person there about the appropriate ratio of waiters to guests so the evening runs smoothly.

A GOOD MAÎTRE D'

When planning a party at a local venue, start with a call to the manager. Ask if he can accommodate you in the area you want to be in, and be specific about this and every other detail thereafter. If you haven't seen the space, check it out in advance. For a more formal affair, do an advance tasting of the meal, including wine and dessert. Confirm that your point person—be it the manager or someone else with clout—will actually be there during the time of your reservation so that a member of staff is accountable for the success of the event.

If it's a sit-down dinner, go with a prix fixe menu. Include a vegetarian option, even if you know you have a carnivorous crew. Someone may not be into pork or is watching his or her calories. Wine, alcohol, and even flowers are usually not part of the menu budget, so work those out in advance, too, along with any time limits. This is where having a relationship with a point person can help immensely.

Dinner is certainly not the only festive option outside the home. Consider a cocktail hour for a birthday or other celebration from 6 to 8 p.m., a late-night meet-and-greet for ice cream sundaes, cake, and berries, or champagne and coffee from ten to midnight. Just be specific about the times, so there's no question among revelers whether a main course is involved.

At the Chateau with Cameron

why entertain at home when a restaurant is at your very service?

Azzaro designer Vanessa Seward

Vanessa Seward is the quintessential Parisian. She is beautiful in an un-Hollywood kind of way, elegantly charming, funny, and chic from head to heel. That she's originally from Argentina only adds to her allure. Designer Loris Azzaro—oft-cited in his heyday as the Parisian Halston—must have seen it when he hired her as his assistant. When he died in 2002, Vanessa succeeded him as creative director of the house of Azzaro, and she's worn the title très bonne. She continues to resurrect the brand to critical success from her mirror-covered atelier on rue du Faubourg Saint-Honoré. Here she answers why she prefers entertaining at a dining table away from home.

I'm not a very good cook. So when it comes to having a dinner party, I will usually opt for a favorite restaurant. There's luxury to this because someone else does all the hard work. That leaves only the most pleasurable part for the host.

It's always great if you know the owner and it's a restaurant that can be intimate, or has an area, maybe a room, that provides an intimacy among your party. At home in Paris, I love Brasserie Wepler at Place de Clichy in the 18th Arrondissement. It is this century-old Paris landmark, the biggest oyster house in all of the city and very old-school with a great history. I like it because of the mix of people—locals, actors, artists. It makes for good people watching. I try to avoid the fashionable place of the moment because it makes some people uneasy or like they have to look good, to perform.

The mix of people at a party is so very important. I don't like to have just fashion people. They should come from many walks of life. It's also good to have a few bachelors. It's always nice if there's a bit of seduction in the air. The best thing for me is if I do a dinner or party and a couple is matched!

As guests arrives, have ready a self-serve champagne stop.

Conversation is as an essential part of the feast.

When I visit Los Angeles, it's wonderful at the Chateau Marmont. I love dining outside, under the Gothic arches, and the manager there always makes sure there are plenty of fragrant flowers, candles, and ashtrays on the table. Like Welper, it has such an infamous history, too!

Last spring Rachel and Cameron from Decades co-hosted a dinner for me there that went very late. For me it was really flattering to see all these beautiful friends dressed in Azzaro, and wearing it in their own way. There was Joy Bryant wearing the tunic with leggings, and China Chow, who immediately stuck the crystal Azzaro comb I gave her in her hair. I gave the combs to the girls, and it's a nice touch to give a little something if there's a celebration involved. It can be something small, but from the heart.

Cohost Cameron Silver

If it's a big dinner, I call ahead and create a set menu. But even with a set menu, at a restaurant you can still order something special for those friends with dietary requests. My dear friend Julie Delpy is allergic to many things and Rachel is a vegetarian. At a restaurant, there's a kind of independence at play, because people can make special requests they might not dare make in a friend's home.

It's also good to have a few appetizers on hand when hungry guests arrive. It's not so much out of concern that the drink may go to their heads too fast. Actually, I don't think it's so bad for the party when people are a bit tipsy.

Always have a lot of champagne ready. It's always very festive and it's perfectly suitable throughout the meal. This way guests don't mix alcohol. If they stick to champagne through the night, they can wake up fresh the next day.

Mischa at ease
in Dior at an
amFAR benefit in
Cannes, 2007.

playing dress up

I'm wild about costume and theme parties. My favorite (okay, no surprise) summons up the spirit of Studio 54. Nicole Richie threw her own disco-rama for her twenty-fourth birthday at the club LAX and called the night "Studio 24." Everyone dressed to the nines. I shimmied into a bright red jersey jumpsuit, draped on the gold chains, put on the gold makeup, and slipped on the gold platforms. Then I realized, this is how I dress every night! Not so Rodger, thankfully, who was game in a nylon print shirt and white poly Angel Flight trousers. Nicole looked incredible in two costume changes for the night: first, a vintage Azzaro dress; later hot pants and a furry vest.

My friends Jacqui and Peter Getty also throw an annual Halloween bash that is considered one of the best anywhere. Part of the reason is the guest list, which can run from Mario Testino and Kate Moss to Kirsten Dunst and Jacqui's sister-in-law Sofia Coppola. Despite the boldface legion crammed into their Hollywood Hills home, however, what makes the late-night event such a screaming success each year is that *everyone* comes in costume. In recent years, Jacqui and Peter appeared as Hamlet and Lady Ophelia; I went as an angel; Kirstie Hume appeared as Marlene Dietrich in *Blue Angel;* no one recognized Chloe Sevigny as an island medicine doctor, all crazy hair and bones; and designer Jeremy Scott appeared as a supersized order of McDonald's French fries.

If an invite lists a theme or dress code, then honor your host and fellow guests by turning it out. It doesn't have to cost much either. Raid a relative's closet, or go treasure hunting in a thrift store. Find a picture of someone you want to emulate, whether it's a real-life retro star or an imagined fantasy character, and have fun with the makeup, jewelry, and clothes.

It can be as simple as choosing a color theme. Take a page out of Truman Capote's diary and hold a black-and-white ball, where everyone is required to come dressed in black and white—masquerade is optional, but it's up to you to decide at invite time. Rose threw a thirtieth birthday all in red, down to the Red Stripe beer, red wine, and choice of red food such as tandoori chicken. Everyone dressed in all shades of red, and the house and backyard were filled with red flowers of every kind and red candles.

Of course, a theme party can be a state of place and plates. With a few makeshift decorative flourishes and a menu tailored to a theme, an otherwise conventional party becomes something else. Or pick a restaurant that is high on camp in its embrace of a culture, real or imagined.

During the warmer months, I love a Moroccan-theme party. It's so summery, so goddessy. We do everything on the ground, seated on throw rugs and pillows, and serve a Moroccan feast along with plenty of chilled white wine sangria and hot mint tea. It also gives me an excuse to let out my inner Talitha Getty and wear one of my treasured Gucci or YSL caftans.

presents of mind

It's your friend's birthday. Or your host is opening her home to you. Do *not* arrive empty-handed.

For life's big moments—an anniversary, a birthday—even a small gift is better than a rain check. Bring your lust for life into your giving by choosing something that celebrates the occasion and the honoree. If the recipients have everything, then consider a donation to a charity in their name. Even $20 can benefit a worthy organization in need, such as the American Red Cross or UNICEF. Or consider a little something from the heart, such as a cherished book or charm necklace, with a handwritten note of what the person means to you.

A guest is never obligated to bring a gift, of course. Being with those you love should never be about obligations. Do it because the entire process makes you and the host tipsy with gratitude for each other.

A decent gift for a host can be a bunch of flowers, mini cupcakes, a scented candle, or certainly a bottle of champagne. But it can be twice the fun to show up with something unexpected like:

- *A photograph of you and the host from another memorable evening. Slip it into a card with a brief message.*

- *A Polaroid camera, loaded and ready to shoot photos you can either toss out to fellow guests or lay out on a side table through the night for everyone to check out at the end of the affair.*

- *A potted herb plant. Mint is great because it's useful in cooking and cocktails.*

- *A blank book for guests to scrawl in what they love about the host. It's a tradition that can continue until the book is filled out.*

Never present a present like it's an Academy Award. Hand it off with a hug and kiss and move on. After all, those hands have to be available for that tube of bubbly on the way.

Molly Sims

Dancing queens!

my thirty-fifth birthday at the hollywood social club

Keira Knightley

mmmm . . .

Rodger and me

Rose

Mary-Kate Olsen and her friend Hayden

chapter 8
glamour a to zoe

we started this party by asking
"Why glamour?"

For me, it's the difference between a life
lived engaged or one spent asleep. But it's not a life
without dreams. It's when we allow ourselves to dream that
we can create a better reality for ourselves—a better career, a
better home, even better memories because we tried a little harder in
the manner we entertained our friends or because we took the cheap red-
eye to visit family.

That's really it. Trying a little harder. Or a lot. I'm not going to
kid you. There *is* something magical about glamour, but it doesn't
just happen with a twitch of the nose or snap of the fingers. You
can't sleep in late every day and expect the good life to happen. In
anything you pursue, you have to be willing to give more than 9–5.
You have to make sacrifices sometimes to chase your dream as hard
as you want it. Passion will bring you success, but it can never, ever
be driven by how sexy the job or lifestyle is, or by the promise of
designer clothes and a flashy car. Those things can be amazing consequences,
but if they are your only reason for pursuing something, you'll likely fail—
whether it's in the job, or, even worse, by failing to truly realize your bona
fide dreams.

Obstacles? They will always be there. There will always be people
you don't get along with, or, worse, who want to knock you down.
There will always be fierce competition. So what? Keep your chin up.
Try not to get tangled up in pettiness. Stay the course. Smile.

Even during the dirtiest moments of my job—and whether
they play out in the press or behind the scenes, there are more than

anyone's fair share—I keep my happy face on. This is not about being fake. It's just being respectful to others. After all, everyone else is not involved in the drama, so I don't see any reason for bringing them down by being bitchy or grumpy. Besides, I find that a smile and graciousness are not just contagious among others, they can also shift my own emotional state and move me beyond the negative.

My father instilled in me at a very young age the idea that work can't always be fun and it can't always be what you want—because it's work. Drama and stress are par for the course. There are going to be days when you wish you could just push the fast-forward button. Repeatedly. But you have to keep a thick skin and rise above it.

My father also taught me at a young age that you don't have to be ruthless and vindictive to succeed. You can be a nice person *and* be successful. Yes, be nice. Shocking advice with some shockingly terrific results. There's certainly no rule inked anywhere that requires diva behavior to work in fashion or Hollywood, contrary to popular opinion. I don't imagine haughty antics play out very well in any field, whether you're an attorney or a zoologist.

Even in my mid-thirties, I still recall lessons my parents taught me (sometimes ad nauseam) and learn new ones every day about others and myself, and the way the world turns. Life can completely be a soap opera at times. So learn and move on. You have to remind yourself of all the loving people in your life, and everything you already have to be grateful for.

I guess that's why even though it's work, I have a ball doing what I do, and not just because I find it creatively necessary. I remember seeing a bumper sticker that read: "The meaning of life is living it." So I do. I live it up in a way I'm passionate about—in full, unabashed, no-holds-barred glamour. I mean, haven't you discovered by now that whenever you up the ante a bit, you enjoy it all even more? It can start as a figment of your imagination. It's a vicarious trip through people and places that inspire you and that you can learn from to make your own. It's something that bends to your desire (and means). It's an exercise in refining, and refining, and then refining some more—much like the job of a stylist.

Each time you find a new place to refine, to style, whether it involves your wardrobe or some other aspect of your world, be fearless.

Your dress—not your life—should hold drama. I love this vintage Dior because it's alive with color and sparkle.

The meaning of life is living it.

idol *speak*

*Utterly fearless in her quest is **Donatella Versace**—the grand dame of bronzed, blonde, and bodacious glamour herself. Asked "Why glamour?" she echoed my reply, and then some. First as muse and now as chief designer for the house her late brother Gianni founded, Donatella epitomizes everything glamour, from the hotels and jets and, of course, fashions bearing the brand's signature gold medusa logo to her own fabulous personal lifestyle. So Donatella, why bother?*

Donatella Versace, the Mighty

Why not? You should live to the best of your abilities and, yes, living glamorously requires effort and time more than money. But I believe it is important to maintain high standards when it comes to taking care of yourself and the way you dress and live—particularly now as the world becomes increasingly informal and lackadaisical.

When I was growing up there were occasions when you simply had to dress up and make an effort—simple things like going to church, traveling on a plane, Sunday lunch with the family. Dressing up gave these occasions a certain importance—it made these little things more glamorous and I miss that. Just think about traveling, how thirty years ago, people wore their best suits and outfits to travel. Now tracksuits are the norm.

Nowadays, you can even wear jeans to most offices, and families don't sit down to eat their meals together. It has nothing to do with money. It simply has to do with the choices you make. Believe me, you certainly won't catch me dead in trainers and a sweatshirt outside the gym. Scruffy is unacceptable.

What makes me feel instantly glamorous? Freshly washed and blow-dried hair. A new lip gloss—not lipstick but gloss—very important! A new handbag or pair of shoes. But I wouldn't describe glamour as a particular object so much as a sensation: the feeling of silk, a glass of champagne, a pair of gold heels.

It doesn't matter what's going on in your life. If you at least make an effort to look your best, and if you keep your surroundings looking good, you will feel a lot better than you would otherwise. Believe me!

The divine DV is absolutely right. Everything glamour begins with a decision. What kind of life do you want? What do you want in life? Even not bothering, just existing according to the status quo, is a choice. And what thrill is there in just being average?

Glamour isn't a dirty word. Don't dismiss it as another word for conspicuous consumption. It isn't going to just happen with a major shopping spree. Glamour is a luxuriant reality marked by charming, unexpected details. It's an upbeat mood sweeping through your day and into the night. It's the pop in your champagne. It's a lifestyle you breathe in deeply and exhale with a celebratory *yippee*!

As trouser options go, a crisp white suit, like this Dolce & Gabbana look on Brittany Murphy, is forever chic.

Yet another snapshot of the ever-radiant Anne Hathaway, this time in Marchesa at the Screen Actors Guild Awards, February 2007

Salma Hayek is among the most beautiful and brainiest women I've had the privilege of knowing, and I always come away from our collaborations feeling all the more inspired and empowered. We've worked together on her look for the Oscars and other events, as well as ad campaigns and editorials. We first met at her home for a fitting in 2004, prepping for the promotional tour for **After the Sunset.** *We connected immediately. Our birthdays are one day apart—mine is September 1, hers is the second—so being Virgos, we're always striving for perfection, always striving for more. Salma has also mastered enjoying her life and balancing that with duty. For her, there's always room to do and be more. Here, Salma explains:*

In the not so distant past, glamour was about being an unapproachable, distant, creature of beauty. To achieve that look required overwhelming artifice in every respect. Today, we've evolved and broadened that concept into a much more modern ideal. It no longer means simply aspiring to be an object to look at, a decoration. For me personally, glamour can mean being strong, professional, elegant, compassionate. Some of the women I find most glamorous are the most proactive about a whole range of issues. They exude a confidence in having a voice of their own.

Going back to the etymology of the word "glamour" was derived from the Latin word "grammatica," meaning scholarship: to learn, to think. During the Middle Ages, it referred to occult learning, the science of using your own inner power, or what we call "magic." To me, this original idea applies equally today. We cast a spell of allure and charm by learning who we are and by expressing ourselves.

Glamour can come from the way you dress, but doesn't mean overthinking and constructing every look. Trying too hard can communicate a lack of confidence. A true sense of style is not just following fashion, but being unique. Having style is understanding the best way to present yourself—because you feel completely comfortable. It is being a participant in the world by contributing to it. It's a whole, well-rounded experience and something to experience completely. To me, that's bewitchingly attractive, that's glamorous. That is learning your own

Salma Hayek in Dior

style a to zoe

a

accessories are central to conveying not only an appearance of glamour, but the feeling of it. Sunglasses, jewelry, purse, and shoes and any other elements you may throw on (a belt? hat? gloves?) that let you stand apart from the rest. This is one indulgence that isn't bad for your health!

b

be unapologetic. Glamour is not a discipline for the meek or modest. It should be enthusiastically embraced. Chin held high, never explain or defend it. It's who you are, after all, and you should never apologize for being your true self.

c

chill champagne, either on the bottom shelf of the refrigerator for a few hours or by placing it in a bucket filled with ice and water for about twenty minutes. If you need it now, toss salt into the bucket. This lowers the temperature below zero. Pour at 43 to 48 degrees Fahrenheit. Never stash it in the freezer; it will affect the alcohol and flavor balance—and your celebration.

d

My Dream Girls: assistants Lia Davis and Taylor Jacobson

dance like it's your last night on earth. In a club with dozens of darling friendly strangers or at home with one strange darling friend, you can get lost in the music and forget all your troubles. Exhausted? Do a little disco and be reborn. You'll be on such a high that you won't feel the pain from the high heels till the morning after. I love to dance! D is also for *dressing up*—always. Every day is another day and another reason for looking fabulous.

e

editing is an ongoing process. Rework a look. Revise your closet or cabinets. Reassemble a room. Don't dress or decorate something for the sake of a trend. If it doesn't inspire you anymore, toss it out. If your gut says it's too much, it most likely is. As a writer friend of mine says, "When in doubt, cut it out."

f

first-class is the way to go. But if you can't actually fork over the funds for front-cabin placement, at least make the journey feel like first-class. Snuggle up in that cashmere wrap you brought along. Have the iPod fully loaded. Create the means for first-class treatment in whatever you do, even if it's just a *frame of mind.*

g

good deeds and a gracious orientation are glamorous. Treating *everyone* with kindness and a smile doesn't require a lot of effort, yet can make all the difference in a person's harried day. G is also for *gutsy.* Dare to take chances, even if it's just baby steps at first. The feeling is liberating—and a buzz.

h

halston is the patron saint of glamour. First as a milliner, the Iowa-born designer created the pillbox hats that crowned First Lady Jacqueline Kennedy. But he streamlined his designs (and his personal style) into a well-tailored, simple, sleek, and utterly glamorous aesthetic that defined the 1970s—and modern fashion forever after. He's Studio 54. He's sexy chic. He's American Style. Halston left this earth at age fifty-eight in 1990. His spirit and impact continue. Look him up. I collect him like crazy. So having a creative role with this legendary brand is as if I'd died and gone to heaven. And as a stylist, I work by his credo: "You're only as good as the people you dress."

Halston returns to Studio 54 at the re-opening gala in 1981.

In one of my treasured vintage Halstons

i

iconic clothes, furniture, and other pieces are always good investments. If it means waiting a little to save up and score, then it's worth it. It's better to have fewer things of quality than too much expendable junk. At times of acquisition, remind yourself that less is indeed more.

j

jewelry should be the last thing you put on and the first thing you take off. Many items such as pearls can be damaged by hair spray or perfume; other items can damage delicate fabrics with their catchy fasteners or settings. That said, for all its precious quality, precious jewelry shouldn't be resigned to special occasions. Real luxury is using the good stuff every day.

k

kissing on the cheek is a wonderful way to greet friends, even new ones. (If some of you guys out there are skittish about kissing another guy, a firm, manly handshake will do.) Lightly touch cheek to cheek or lips to cheek. Repeat with the other cheek. It's a quick action. In the U.S., a single kiss is enough. In Paris, it's four with the sequence starting left cheek first. In Madrid, two is plenty, starting with the right side. As for London? The Brits are just warming up to physical contact from strangers, so in many cases a nod and informal "hi" will do.

l

live it up, and *love* and *laugh* with abandon, too. An open heart is contagious. Everything is better for it.

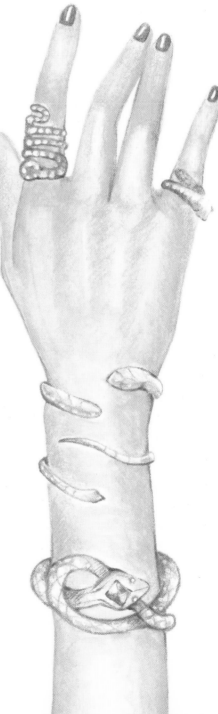

a day in the life of a stylist, paris 2006

Meet the press:
back to back with
Harvey Weinstein

Liv Tyler
backstage
at Dior

Line-up at Dior couture show

On stage, post-show with Mischa Barton

Hero worship: with Galliano!

Post-show dinner with John Galliano, Drew Barrymore,
Jacquetta Wheeler, Margherita Missoni, and other pals

m

make a statement. Bring focus to a room or dinner table with a decorative accessory.
And give your personal look some interest with a single piece that is uniquely you. It can be two
statements, but don't overdo it. Too much information looks like a mess. And never, ever do it at
the risk of trying too hard.

n

nails should be clipped and clean. Dragon lady claws are only good if you're playing the dragon lady.
Lacquer shades of red, or a wine or a deep berry that's nearly black look particularly chic on short
(but not nail-bitten length!) fingernails and toenails. But keep remover close: if polish smudges, dab
a wet fingertip from the opposite hand and gently blend away; when polish is noticeably chipped,
remove it completely. You're better off neat and nude.

o

orchids are beautifully delicate, simply modern—
and much easier to care for than you would think. Unlike
starlets, orchids can go days, even weeks, without being
fussed over. There are a bazillion kinds of orchids, and as
long as you know what each one likes in terms of water,
light, feeding, and so on, you can keep one beyond the next
fashion season cycle. When it comes to sending flowers
they're also so much chicer than roses.

p

P is for *peacock*—or *polished*—as in the well-dressed man.
Nothing is sexier. Even a cheap suit can look better if it is tailored
and paired with good quality shoes. Play with a colored shirt or
socks. Scarves, ascots, or cuff links are another point of play. A touch
of jewelry can work, too. Be a peacock, but never show up your
boss—or even worse, your woman.

q

Use *q-tips* or other cotton swabs to keep lip color at bay: dip it in loose face powder and apply at the outer lip edge. If you can't find your lip pencil, roll the end of the swab into a point between your forefinger and thumb. Run the newly created point on the side of the lipstick. Apply with the pointed tip like a pencil; then fill in with the lipstick. If any color does bleed beyond the lip line, dab the swab in makeup remover and carefully wipe off.

r

round bandages are a quick and inexpensive way to cover up those headlights for nipples. Consult your medicine cabinet for other quick fixes. Preparation H is an instant way to dab away the puffiness under the eyes. And a touch of Neosporin at the nostril's edge is a good way to keep germs at bay on flights.

s

seduction is a big part of glamour. Many of the iconic women we adore have an element of seduction about them that seems to work its magic even from photographs: Sophia Loren, Brigitte Bardot, Lauren Hutton, Bianca Jagger. It's more of a suggestion in the eyes or mannerisms. A flash of leg or shoulder can do it, too. Seduction is not to be confused with blatantly slutty overtures. I mean, there's nothing seductive about an exposed midsection unless you're a belly dancer.

Rebecca Romijn looking like a goddess personified in Gucci

t

thank-you notes are not an option. They are mandatory. While a handwritten note is preferred, a thank you in any form—a phone call, an e-mail, or even a text message if you truly can't interrupt the chaos in your life to sit down and pen a note—is better than none at all. Everyone likes to feel appreciated.

u

undone glamour is modern. A look too buttoned-up, too polished, is not only dated, it's also boring. A gorgeous over-the-top gown begs for a messy chignon. Think Kate Moss, who can mix high and low and tweak formal like no one else.

v

vintage is more popular than ever, making it a bit tougher at times to get a good deal. But it's usually a better score than something new—the price could be as much as a third of the original tag, and it's all the better if it means being the only one at the party in that particular dress. The cycle of life continues, too. You can usually resell vintage, especially if the provenance or quality is good.

Glamour shouldn't vanish with pregnancy or other figure changes. Just like Kate Hudson in this simple, strapless Chanel, always celebrate your womanly curves.

W

white wine is good as more than an accompaniment to fish. It's also great for bleaching out red wine stains. Follow up with soda water to remove the residue.

X

Marks some of life's greatest pleasures—*luxe, sex, excess,* and *extra.* A great way to start any word, as in extra chic!

y

you are anyone you want to become. It might take getting out of bed an hour earlier, and hitting the pillow an hour later. It might mean being flexible with your dreams to make them a reality. It might require a sacrifice now for gains later. In the end, it's up to you.

Z

Well, it's for *zoe,* of course. It's much easier to spell than Rosenzweig, so it's my surname de facto. Despite rumors, it really is my middle name and it rhymes with "oh." Got that? What's in a name, anyway, but the person who claims it? Remember, a good life, a life of everything glamour, is told best over chilled bubbly, among people you adore, and knowing that you gave it your all.

A night I will always remember: the opportunity to dress the great glamazon Mary J. Blige.

acknowledgments

High, high heels firmly dug into a world more noted for its superficialities than its heart, we want to recognize the intensely enthusiastic support, assistance, and generosity we received in making this book happen from so many dear friends from Hollywood to Milan.

There are, of course, the incredible women Rachel gets to dress and be inspired by on a daily basis. They are her raison d'etre for this book ever coming about. We especially thank the amazing individuals—clients, designers and image makers—whose contributions transformed this into more than just another style guide: Mischa Barton, Joy Bryant, Roberto Cavalli, Francisco Costa, Alberta Ferretti, Valentino Garavani, Jennifer Garner, Pamela Glassman, Anne Hathaway, Salma Hayek, Michael Kors, Andy LeCompte, Tamara Mellon, Margherita Missoni, Amy Sacco, Vanessa Seward, Cameron Silver, Molly Sims, Paul Starr, Donatella Versace, Diane von Furstenberg, and Frank Zambrelli.

Our jobs, however, both in life and within these covers, owe much to the extraordinary individuals who connect us quickly and no matter what time it is with the brilliant designers and gorgeous fashion that are a cornerstone of our work. To them, we give a big, big thank you for coping with our deadlines and ceaselessly delivering: Maddalena Aspes (Missoni), Malcolm Carfrae and Denise Corcoran (Calvin Klein), Billy Daley (Kors), Carlo Mengucci and Cristiano Mancini (Cavalli), Andreas Mercante (Ferretti), Salome Nortey (Versace), Alexis Rodriguez (DVF), Sarah Posen (Zac Posen), Nicole Simithraaratchy (Leiber), Carlos Souza and Silvia Angioletti (Valentino), Marie de Saint Steban (Azzaro), and Jason Weisenfeld. So, too, their counterparts in Hollywood: Kira Dominguez (Hayek) and Michael Hathaway.

Ever magnanimous with their time, assistance and insight have been Nanci Ryder, Leslie Sloane, Brad Caffareli, Steven Huvane, Harvey Weinstein, Georgina Chapman, the Chateau Marmont family, Jason Pomerenac and the 60 Thompson Hotel family, Jenni Kayne, the Decades team, and Katy Rodriguez and Mark Haddawy and their Resurrection crew. As a stylist and as a writer, we shine brightest thanks in large part to those who have turned up the spotlight on Rachel's achievements: Glenda Bailey, Charla Lawhon, Roberta Myers, Carine Roitfeld, Hal Rubenstein, Linda Wells, Anna Marie Wilson, and James Fallon.

Everyone appreciates a great finale, and we had to save the best for last. It's to those behind the scenes—to the entire Zoe Camp—where our gratitude is immeasurable: Lia Davis, Taylor Jacobson, George Clinton, Brandy St. John, as well as Byron Williams, Lori Schizas from Magnet, Todd Shemarya, Heather Devlin, and, in particular, the ever charming, ever patient Parke Steiger. The Zoe Camp grew with this project, and we wish to also express our loving thanks to Donato Sardella— who always ensures we look good; Blanca Apodaca—for coming to the rescue; and Jeff Vespa, Justin Weiss, Alice Jordan-Licht, Justin Tables, and the other talented folks at WireImage. Thank you, too, to Natalie Kaire and Kallie Shimek at Grand Central Publishing; as well as our champion and editor, Rebecca Isenberg, who managed to remain adrenalized and always sunny throughout this project.

We kiss you all!

—rachel and rose

photography and illustration credits

Endpaper left: Rachel Zoe and Kate Beckinsale; Cameron Diaz; Mischa Barton with dog; Mischa Barton; Molly Sims; Rachel Zoe in white dress by Donato Sardella/WireImage.com. Jennifer Garner; Rebecca Romijn; Demi Moore and Lindsay Lohan by Steve Granitz/WireImage.com. Maria Sharapova by Rachel Zoe. Rachel Zoe and her family by Ron Rosenzweig. All others by Donato Sardella. Endpaper right: Mischa Barton and Rachel Zoe (black dress) by Billy Farrell/PatrickMcMullan.com. At clothing rack by Dimitrios Kambouris/WireImage.com. Cameron Diaz by Lalo Yasky/WireImage.com. Rachel Zoe and Mischa Barton (red dress); With Liv Tyler by Rodger Berman. Salma Hayek; Lindsay Lohan; jewelry by Rachel Zoe. Rachel Zoe's parents; Rodger and nephew; with Rodger; Rachel in sunglasses from Rosenzweig Archives. All others by Donato Sardella. Page viii: Bianca Jagger and Halston celebrate her birthday, 1980; by Ron Galella/WireImage.com. Page 3: top, Ron Rosenzweig; bottom, RJ Capak/WireImage.com. Page 4: top, Rachel Zoe; bottom, Brian Ach/WireImage.com. Page 5: left, Eric Charbonneau/WireImage.com; right, Michael Caulfield/WireImage.com. Page 6: Ron Rosenzweig. Page 7: top left, Rosenzweig Archives; others, Ron Rosenzweig. Page 9: Randy Brooke/WireImage.com. Page 10: sketches, clockwise from top, courtesy of Michael Kors, Azzaro, and Giambattista Valli. Page 11: Donato Sardella/WireImage.com. Page 12: Rachel Zoe. Page 13: clockwise from top left, Rosenzweig Archives, Dimitrios Kambouris/WireImage.com, Patrick McMullan/PatrickMcMullan.com, Ron Rosenzweig, Rosenzweig Archives. Page 17: Donato Sardella/WireImage.com. Page 18: Donato Sardella. Page 21: John Sciulli/WireImage.com. Page 22: Alexandra Wyman/WireImage.com. Page 23: Donato Sardella/WireImage.com. Page 25: left, Jim Spellman/WireImage.com; right, Donato Sardella/WireImage.com. Page 29: Billy Farrell/PatrickMcMullan.com. Page 32: Marc Susset-Lacroix/WireImage.com. Page 34: Donato Sardella/WireImage.com. Page 36: Lester Cohen/WireImage.com. Page 37: Billy Farrell/PatrickMcMullan.com. Page 39: Courtesy of Leiber. Page 40: James Devaney/WireImage.com. Page 42: Keira Knightley shines in Gucci; by Tomos Brangwyn/WireImage.com. Page 45: Jeffrey Mayer/WireImage.com. Page 46: Tony Barson/WireImage.com. Page 47: James Devaney/WireImage.com. Page 48: Steve Granitz/WireImage.com. Page 50: Donato Sardella. Page 51: Dimitrios Kambouris/WireImage.com. Page 52: Rachel Zoe. Page 53: Steve Granitz/WireImage.com. Page 55: Rodger Berman. Page 56: Jeff Vespa/WireImage.com. Page 59: Donato Sardella/WireImage.com. Page 63: Patrick McMullan/PatrickMcMullan.com. Page 64: Sketches courtesy and copyright Michael Kors. Page 66: Victor Chavez/WireImage.com. Page 69: Jeffrey Mayer/WireImage.com. Page 70: Courtesy of Alberta Ferretti. Page 71: Donato Sardella/WireImage.com. Page 73: Dimitrios Kambouris/WireImage.com. Page 75: Kevin Mazur/WireImage.com. Page 76: At work with an oversized bag and in the amazing vintage YSL coat my mother scored at a flea market; by Jamie McCarthy/WireImage.com. Page 81: James Devaney/WireImage.com. Page 82: Carmen Valdes/WireImage.com. Page 83: Donato Sardella/WireImage.com. Page 84: left, Lalo Yasky/WireImage.com; right, Theo Wargo/WireImage.com. Page 85: Richard Lewis/WireImage.com. Pages 86–87: Jamie McCarthy/WireImage.com. Page 89: Billy Farrell/PatrickMcMullan.com. Page 90: John Furniss/WireImage.com. Page 92: View from the boat in Cannes; by Rodger Berman. Page 95: Jamie McCarthy/WireImage.com. Pages 96–97: top left, Rachel Zoe; others by Rodger Berman. Page 98: John Parra/WireImage.com. Page 99: Jeff Vespa/WireImage.com. Page 100: Rosenzweig Archives. Page 103: Djamilla Rosa Cochran/WireImage.com. Page 104: James Devaney/WireImage.com. Page 108: Mischa being made up; courtesy of Paul Starr. Page 111: top, Billy Farrell/PatrickMcMullan.com; bottom, Rachel Zoe. Page 112: left and top, Donato Sardella/WireImage.com; bottom right, Rachel Zoe. Pages 113–114: courtesy of Paul Starr. Page 116: Stephen Lovekin/WireImage.com. Page 118: Rachel Zoe. Page 119: Rosenzweig Archives. Page 122: Donato Sardella. Page 124: Donato Sardella/WireImage.com. Page 125: Steve Granitz/WireImage.com. Page 126: Rachel and Rodger on their patio; by Donato Sardella. Page 131: Donato Sardella. Page 132: Tony Barson/WireImage.com. Pages 133–141: Donato Sardella. Page 143: Billy Farrell/PatrickMcMullan.com. Page 144–146: Donato Sardella. Page 148: Keira Knightley in Herve Leger; by Jon Furniss/WireImage.com. Page 151: Foc Kan/WireImage.com. Page 152: top, Donato Sardella/WireImage.com; others, Rodger Berman. Page 155: Nick Harvey/WireImage.com. Page 156: Barry King/WireImage.com. Pages 157–159: Donato Sardella/WireImage.com. Page 160: Jeff Vespa/WireImage.com. Pages 162–163: cake, Rodger Berman; bottom row middle, Andy Griffith; all others, Donato Sardella. Page 164: With Tom Ford, by Erik T. Kaiser/PatrickMcMullan.com. Page 167: Chance Yeh/PatrickMcMullan.com. Page 168: Rabbani Solimene Photography/WireImage.com. Page 169: left, Kevin Mazur/WireImage.com; right, Steve Granitz/WireImage.com. Page 170: Steve Granitz/WireImage.com. Page 171: top, Ryan Born/WireImage.com; bottom, Rachel Zoe. Page 172: top, Ron Galella/WireImage.com; bottom, Donato Sardella/WireImage.com. Pages 174–175: bottom left, Tony Barson/WireImage.com; others by Rodger Berman. Page 177: John Sciulli/WireImage.com. Page 178: Jim Spellman/WireImage.com. Page 179: Jeff Vespa/WireImage.com.

about the authors

RACHEL ZOE is the go-to force among A-list actresses, fashion houses, beauty firms and magazine editors seeking a dose of her signature effortlessly chic style, which has been heralded by *W, Vogue, Harper's Bazaar,* the *New York Times, Los Angeles Times,* and *London Times,* and fashion bible *Women's Wear Daily* as influencing the tenor and face of fashion. She was recently appointed to the advisory board of Halston as creative consultant, and she designed a luxury bag collection under her name for Leiber. Zoe orchestrates the look of campaigns for Jimmy Choo, Tag Heuer, Motorola, and Bebe; and of editorial stories for a roster of international fashion magazines. She is the recipient of the Fashion Group International 2006 Fashion Oracle Award; the Accessories Council Fashion Influencer Ace Award; and ranked on several lists among the most influential women in Hollywood and internationally.

Zoe sees beyond trends to what looks best on the women she works with—Cameron Diaz, Salma Hayek, Keira Knightley, Lindsay Lohan, Mischa Barton, Jennifer Garner, Kate Beckinsale, Liv Tyler, and Anne Hathaway. Born Rachel Zoe Rosenzweig, the New York native parlayed majors in sociology and psychology into styling some of the world's biggest stars. Zoe and her husband, venture capitalist Rodger Berman, now reside full time in Los Angeles.

ROSE APODACA is well regarded as an authority of California and Hollywood style and its billion-dollar industry. Her features have appeared in *Harper's Bazaar, Glamour, Elle, Los Angeles Times Magazine, W,* Style.com, and her blog on Uber.com. She was consulting editor of the successful launch of the *Los Angeles Times* section Image and prior to that helmed the West Coast bureau of *Women's Wear Daily,* where she upped the coverage of the red carpet, apparel, and beauty businesses based there. Her nearly two decades covering the region, from hard news to pop culture, led to a renewed focus from international fashion designers and the press, and the formal establishment of Los Angeles Fashion Week. She is regularly tapped by media outlets, and taught college-level fashion writing and history. Apodaca's influence was recognized at the inaugural Los Angeles Fashion Awards.

Besides stakes in Beauty Bar Hollywood and Las Vegas, she and husband, Andrew Griffith, own the global modern design shops, e-commerce site, and consultancy A+R in the Los Angeles neighborhood of Silver Lake, where they reside.